ERNIE
HARWELL

BREAKING
90

Credits

Editor . . . . .Kevin Bull
Designer . . . . .Ryan Ford
Copy editors . . . . .Bill Collison, David Darby, Jeff
Juterbock, Tim Marcinkoski and
the Free Press sports staff
Photo editor . . . . .Diane Weiss
Cover and back cover photos . . . . .Eric Seals
Photo imaging . . . . .Kathryn Trudeau
Project coordinator . . . . .Dave Robinson
Sports editor . . . . .Gene Myers
Assistant managing editor/presentation . .Steve Dorsey
Special thanks . . . . .Kristin Bull, John Lowe and
A.J. Hartley

Detroit Free Press

615 W. Lafayette St.
Detroit, MI 48226

©2007 by Detroit Free Press. All rights reserved.

Manufactured by Malloy Inc.

OTHER FREE PRESS BOOKS BY ERNIE HARWELL

- Ernie Harwell: Life After Baseball
- Ernie Harwell: Stories from My Life in Baseball

OTHER FREE PRESS TIGERS BOOKS

- Century of Champions
- The Corner
- Corner to Copa
- Roar Restored

To order any of these titles, go to **www.freep.com/bookstore** or call **800-245-5082.**

Dedication

To Richard Whitmer, Daniel Loepp, Rick Cole and Bill Elwell — all great friends and supporters.

Table of contents

Introduction

BY JOHN LOWE

E rnie Harwell is turning 90. He has been around longer than the medium by which we have come to love him.

That medium is commercial radio, which started in this country in the early 1920s. Ernie was born in 1918, the same year as another pair of maestros, Ted Williams and Leonard Bernstein. It was the year in which Babe Ruth began to turn from a pitcher into an outfielder but still helped from the mound as the Red Sox won their last world title of the 20th Century.

Ernie had made his way onto the radio by 1940 in Atlanta. It was then and there that he interviewed Philadelphia A's owner-manager Connie Mack, who was born during the Civil War.

Mack was still running the A's in 1948, when Ernie began his 55-year run as a major league broadcaster. Ernie has continued to write about baseball for the Free Press since he stopped doing Tigers games. Thus either he or Mack has had a hand in every major league season since modern baseball began in 1901.

We might think of Sparky Anderson now like Mack in 1940 — a senior baseball man who has been around about as long as anyone. But the year that Sparky was born, Ernie started writing for

The Sporting News. That was 1934, the year of the first Tigers-Cardinals World Series.

Ernie broadcast the second Tigers-Cardinals World Series in 1968. And in 2006, his column appeared in the Free Press during the third Tigers-Cardinals World Series.

Ernie is still writing beautifully. He tells us stuff almost nobody knows but that everybody can enjoy, because he makes it all so clear and concise.

Here's looking forward to what he writes during the next Tigers-Cardinals World Series.

Ernie's first story in the Free Press

Ernie Harwell has written a baseball column regularly for the Detroit Free Press since 1991. His very first Free Press story was published Feb. 21, 1943, and it appears below:

A rugged ballplayer with 17 years of diamond service ordinarily wouldn't be termed a rookie. Especially, one who has been connected with 14 different clubs, four of them big-league outfits. A player who for five seasons has managed in a high minor league and developed many stars for the big time.

No, ordinarily, such a player wouldn't be called a rookie. But this is war. And Paul Rapier Richards, new Detroit Tiger catcher, will be a war-time rookie when he reports to manager Steve O'Neill for spring training.

Richards will bring with him a record which should make him a valuable newcomer to the Tiger ranks. Not only as a backstop, but also as a strategist and a developer of young stars, especially pitchers.

If you think that Richards will pull himself into the Tiger offices in a wheelchair, forget it right now. Despite his full page in the record book of experience, Paul is only 35 years old, as he started in the National Pastime in 1926 at the age of 17, breaking in with Pittsfield, Mass.

His service with the Tigers will mark Paul's fifth

trip to the big leagues. In 1928 he was the property of the St. Louis Browns. Brooklyn gave him two trials, one in 1931, the other in '32. Paul's longest big league stay was with the New York Giants from '33 through '35. From there he went to the Athletics and finished the 1936 season with Atlanta in the Southern League. He starred with the Crackers as a catcher for two seasons, then he managed the team for the next five, winning two pennants.

His only weakness, the thing that prevented Richards from becoming a top major league performer, is his light stick-work.

Where Richards should be a very valuable asset to Detroit is in his astute handling of pitchers. Hurlers who had no success under other managers found something new and vitalizing when they worked for Richards.

Richards came to the Atlanta club the same year another veteran of many minor league seasons and major league trials — Dutch Leonard — joined them. The Dutchman had been bouncing around the minors for years, never getting anywhere. His fastball was about as speedy as Ernie Lombardi; his curve had no more wrinkle than a pane of glass. But in Atlanta he clicked. For there Leonard found a catcher who could handle the pitch which very few backstops had handled — his knuckle or butterfly ball. The pitch has often been called a "catcher killer." Naturally, most of the backstops didn't relish calling for it often. Richards was different.

Using his knuckler to advantage, Leonard turned

in two fine seasons with Atlanta and won himself a spot in the big time with the Senators.

Richards gave other pitchers the same push. Take for instance Tom Sunkel and Bill Beckmann. When he joined the Crackers in 1938, Sunkel had been pitching in organized ball for six years. Two years before, he had won only six and lost 26 for Asheville. In '38 he captured 21 and dropped just five decisions at Atlanta. He topped the loop in strikeouts and in the earned-run column. So, Tom, on the strength of the work he had done for Richards, went back to the Cards. Now, of course, he is with the New York Giants.

Beckmann had been around even longer than Sunkel when Richards gave him the treatment. Bill began in 1927. With 11 years of mediocre pitching behind him, none in any league higher than the Senators, he won 20 games for Atlanta in '38. After that, he belonged to Connie Mack. It was Richards' clever handling which gave him his big-league opportunity.

In '40, Richards helped develop two more hurlers, Luman Harris and Herman Besse, both still with the Athletics. This last campaign saw another Richards development in Jimmy Mertz. In his first year with the Crackers, Mertz came along fast enough to be drafted this fall by the Senators.

So, it seems that Richards has helped many a young pitcher — and some older ones, too — along the road to big-league prosperity. At Detroit, he'll have a chance to help a number of them in their post-graduate work.

FOR OPENERS

ERNIE ON COMING TO DETROIT IN 1960:

I went to Detroit. It was probably the best move that I ever made, because I stayed there awhile, and I really appreciated the great love and affection that the people of Michigan have shown me over the years.

DISC 3, ERNIE HARWELL'S AUDIO SCRAPBOOK

Home opener is always joyous

O pening Day in Detroit is my favorite civic celebration. It's a true rite of spring when we come together with a festive community spirit. No other sport celebrates its openers like baseball. And only two cities — Detroit and Cincinnati — turn their celebrations into such joyous occasions.

The first Tigers opener I covered was in 1954. I came to Briggs Stadium that afternoon, Tuesday, April 13, not as a Tigers announcer, but as the radio-TV voice of the Baltimore Orioles. The game was not only the Birds' first of the season, it was the first game in the history of Baltimore baseball.

In those days, the Tigers' home opener had not developed into the current all-day party. There was no conglomeration of TV trucks and radio vans surrounding the stadium and no raucous parading in the streets around the ballpark.

Steve Gromek, the 34-year-old Hamtramck native, beat the Orioles, 3-0, with a seven-hitter. The Tigers' runs came on home runs by Ray Boone, Walter Dropo and rookie Frank Bolling off Don Larsen.

That was my first visit to Detroit, but it started a long string of Opening Days here. My next Detroit opener came April 22, 1960, my first season with the Tigers. It was about 80 degrees that afternoon, one of the warmest openers in history. The Tigers beat Chicago, 6-5, but my most vivid memory is the embarrassment George Kell and I suffered in our pregame TV interview with White Sox second baseman Nellie Fox. The taped interview went well, but after it was over, our director told us there had been a flaw in the recording. So, we asked Nellie to do it again. We redid the interview, but again, some kind of mechanical blip ruined it. Fox was a perfect gentleman throughout the fiasco, but George and I spent the whole afternoon wiping egg off our faces.

That warm opener in 1960 was a vivid contrast to the first one in Comerica Park, April 11, 2000. That afternoon was the coldest, most miserable weather I had ever encountered at a baseball game. For a while, it seemed doubtful the game would be played, but the Tigers went on with it because it was the first game at Comerica Park. Commissioner Bud Selig and other dignitaries had traveled to Detroit to be part of the ceremony.

Despite snow and freezing drizzle, the stands were packed — at least at the start of the game. But by the third inning, two-thirds of the crowd had found somewhere to thaw out their chilled bones.

The Tigers rewarded those loyalists who stayed with a 5-2 victory over the Seattle Mariners.

Hot or cold, it's always great to be at Opening Day in Detroit.

ORIGINALLY PRINTED APRIL 11, 2006.

BASEBALL STORIES

 ERNIE ON BASEBALL: Baseball is the president tossing out the first ball of the season. And a scrubby schoolboy playing catch with his dad on the Mississippi farm. A tall, thin, old man waving a scorecard from the corner of his dugout. That's baseball. **99**

DISC 4, ERNIE HARWELL'S AUDIO SCRAPBOOK

A little sweat and flexibility lands job

Many young college graduates dream of working for a Major League Baseball team. Each dreamer asks, "How do I get started?"

Here's the answer from a successful baseball executive, Dave Dombrowski, president and general manager of the Tigers.

Dombrowski had that same dream while attending Western Michigan. His quest started with his undergraduate thesis, "The GM, the Man in the Middle."

"I mailed questionnaires to all the major league general managers," Dombrowski said. "My final question was: Where is the best place to find a job?" Several GMs wrote back with the same suggestion, "Go to baseball's winter meetings and get some interviews."

Dombrowski flew to the meetings in Honolulu in December 1977. There he met Chicago White Sox GM Roland Hemond.

"I might have something for you," Hemond told him. "Meet me in my room tomorrow."

Dombrowski met with Hemond, Charles Evranian (assistant director of player development) and Charlie's boss, Paul Richards. After a two-hour discussion, Hemond promised to phone Dombrowski the next day at 3 p.m. The call came earlier than expected — at 1:30. Dombrowski had just returned from the beach when the phone rang.

"Dave, it's Roland," Hemond said. "Come on up to my room."

"I'm getting into the shower," Dave answered. "Can I make it in about an hour? I'm sweaty and covered with dirt and sand."

"No, Dave. Come now, as you are."

Hemond told Dombrowski he liked his background and asked him to visit him and other club officials the following week in Chicago. A week later, with final exams done, Dombrowski flew from Western Michigan in Kalamazoo to his hometown of Chicago. At Comiskey Park, Hemond introduced him to Rudy Schaffer, White Sox business manager; Mike Veeck, marketing and sales director; and the owner himself, Bill Veeck. The Sox offered Dombrowski the job of administrative assistant in player development and scouting.

"That meant I was a gofer," Dombrowski recalls. "I did everything. I filed, typed letters and picked up visitors at the airport."

A year later, Evranian left the White Sox, and Dombrowski became assistant director of player development and scouting under Richards. At 22, Dombrowski was the only person (besides Richards) in the club's scouting and development department. He was on his way to a successful big-league career.

ORIGINALLY PRINTED JUNE 14, 2004.

Comeback stories are inspiring

Everybody loves a comeback story, and there are plenty in the final weeks of a baseball season. Most comeback stories delineate improvement from the previous year. But two of the bright ones in 2004 highlight in-season surges.

Derek Jeter, who has become Mr. Yankee of the 21st Century, was batting .189 on May 15. He finished the regular season hitting .292, with a career-high 44 doubles and 23 home runs, one short of his best in a season. On the other coast, Seattle's Ichiro Suzuki was batting .255 at the end of April. Sports Illustrated, among others, was bemoaning his demise and predicting a sad season for him. Instead, he became one of the stories of the year with his chase after George Sisler's record of 257 hits in a season. Suzuki finished with 262 hits and a .372 batting average.

The National League can point to a double comeback from two former Tigers. Jose Lima and Jeff Weaver, pitching for the Dodgers, finished the season with a combined total of 26 victories. It's a refreshing change for two who have struggled over the past years.

Another former American Leaguer who found himself in 2004 was Jaret Wright, a refugee from baseball's ash heap. Jaret had great years with

KIRTHMON F. DOZIER

Ernie Harwell shares a moment with Mariners star Ichiro Suzuki at Comerica Park in 2001. Suzuki wanted to meet Harwell.

Cleveland at the start of his career. Then came two shoulder separations and a four-year setback. In 2004, a healthy and mature Wright was one of the Atlanta Braves' best starters, with a 15-8 record and a 3.28 ERA.

ORIGINALLY PRINTED SEPT. 27, 2004.

Bragan, 87, manages to make history

One of my favorite guys has broken a long-standing record. Bobby Bragan replaced Connie Mack as the oldest manager in pro baseball history when he masterminded the Ft. Worth Cats for one game in 2005.

When Bragan, 87, took the job, he was eight days older than Mack, who managed his last game for the Philadelphia A's in 1950.

In his temporary assignment Aug. 16, Bragan displayed the same flair for showmanship that sparked his playing and managing career. For his pregame conference with the umpires, he brought a seeing-eye dog. In the third inning, Bobby was ejected by umpire Brandon Misun. He had asked Misun why he had tossed David Keesee, a Ft. Worth player.

"Because he said I was calling a bad game," Misun said.

"You were calling a bad game," Bragan told him.

Bragan was back in his old form. In his 12-year managing career, he got the thumb an average of six times a season — many times because of innovative methods of protest.

His most famous protest came when managed the Pirates. He strolled onto the field, sipping orange juice through a straw, and offered a drink to the umpires. In the minors, he was even bolder. At Hollywood, he sent his batboy to coach third base. Another time, Bragan stripped off his uniform to protest his ejection. And once he sent eight straight pinch-hitters to bat for one of his players, only one of them — the last — sticking around the plate long enough to take a swing.

Bragan's eccentricities weren't limited to umpire confrontations. With a terrible team at Pittsburgh, he experimented with putting his best hitter in the leadoff spot. He also set up a five-man infield to defend against a bunt situation.

Bragan started his major league career with the Phillies in 1940. He stayed three years as a shortstop, third baseman, second baseman and catcher. He was with Brooklyn in 1943-44 and 1947-48. When Roy Campanella was promoted to the Dodgers in mid-'48, Bobby was sent to Ft. Worth, where he began to manage. In the majors, he managed Pittsburgh, Cleveland, Milwaukee and Atlanta. Later, he became president of the Ft. Worth team, president of the Texas League and finally the National Association of Professional Baseball Leagues.

When I visited Texas with the Tigers, I always enjoyed being with Bragan. It was fun to swap Branch Rickey stories and to hear him play the piano in the press room. When the folks in Texas honored me with a lunch in my final visit there, Bragan was one of the speakers and touched me with his kind remarks.

It's good to see that a guy who loves the game so much is still around, breaking records.

ORIGINALLY PRINTED SEPT. 5, 2005.

Cubs' low-key voice carries well

In the 1980s, Len Kasper was one of the thousands of youngsters playing high school baseball in the United States.

Today he is an outstanding success in one of baseball's prized television jobs with the Chicago Cubs.

When Len pitched and played third base for Shepherd High School, his team got only as far as the state semifinals. In 2005, Kasper, at age 34, hit the heights with his easy, laid-back style on Chicago powerhouse WGN.

Although he paid his dues with early struggles at a lower level, Len's rise to the big leagues was rapid. After starting as a public-address announcer for high school football, the Mt. Pleasant native landed a part-time job at age 17 at WMMI Radio in Shepherd.

Len continued his career in college, broadcasting basketball on the student station at Marquette University. His first pro work was at WISN, Milwaukee, where he was morning sports anchor. After moving to another Milwaukee station, WTMJ, he applied for a spot with the Brewers, but he had no baseball broadcast experience. So he tested himself, working with Brett Dolan on weekend games of the Beloit (Wis.) Brewers of the Midwest League. Tapes of these broadcasts won him a TV debut with the Brewers, where he worked three seasons. He then became the TV voice of the Florida Marlins in 2002-04. In 2005 Kasper won new respect as the Cubs' TV play-by-play man, working with analyst Bob Brenly.

Len lives in Chicago with his wife, Pam, and their son, Leo.

"I'm happy to be back in the Midwest," he says. "Chicago is great. My sister Amy lives here, and it's much easier to get back to Shepherd to see my mom and dad."

It was Len's dad who inculcated in him a love for baseball. They enjoyed following the Tigers together. Len's first Tigers recollection dates to those teams in the late 1970s, when the franchise was building toward the 1984 championship.

During his journey from Shepherd High to the big time, Kasper dabbled in music, playing bass in a couple of four-piece rock bands — the Indentured Servants and the Knowledge.

Now he and Brenly rock and roll with the Cubs.

"Bob's a great guy to work with. I felt comfortable with him from the start," Kasper says.

Len believes "the game is the thing." And he likes to give breathing room to his audience.

"The people here have been great to me," he says. "I appreciate how helpful all of them have been."

It has been a great summer for the onetime pitcher and third baseman from Shepherd. I have a feeling he'll be in Chicago as the TV voice of the Cubs for a long time.

ORIGINALLY PRINTED SEPT. 12, 2005.

Leyland needs no smoke screen

Tigers manager Jim Leyland has two addictions — winning and smoking. His smoking has focused almost as much attention on Leyland as his winning.

Several years ago, the topic came up during a Leyland interview with Chris Myers on ESPN. Leyland cited the usual objections against the habit. Then he paused and said: "But you smokers out there, you all know how we like that special moment after a big meal when you light up and inhale down deep. You know the feeling. Sometimes, smoking is fantastic."

That's classic Leyland — straightforward, candid and no worries about political correctness.

Another well-known smoker in baseball was Charlie Hough. A knuckleball pitcher, Hough pitched 25 years in the big leagues, finishing with a 216-216 record. Like most knuckleballers, Hough didn't have the physique of a male model, but he did work out on an indoor bike. Once, before a game, Hough was pumping on his bike and smoking a cigarette.

"I got to give it up," he said.

"What, the cigarette?" his companion asked.

"No," Hough said. "The bike."

Baseball's most famous smoker was Joe

DiMaggio. Joe always asked the clubhouse boy to bring him a cigarette and a cup of coffee to the Yankees' dugout between innings.

Then there was Earl Weaver, an inveterate smoker. When a pitcher's ineffectiveness would drive the super-nervous manager to sneak another smoke in the dugout, he would say: "This guy is going from a pack-and-a-half pitcher to a two-packer."

Times have changed. Only a few current managers or players are smokers. On teams in the 1940s and '50s, you could find only one or two players who didn't smoke.

When I broadcast for the New York Giants in the 1950s, our sponsor, Chesterfield, gave me a long list of players who endorsed the company's cigarette. If a player made an outstanding play, I had to identify him as a Chesterfield man. However, there were two lists. One contained names of players who actually smoked Chesterfields. I would say: "Yes, Sal Maglie smokes Chesterfields." The other list was tricky. It comprised non-smokers. About them (because of legal regulations), I would have to say: "Al Dark says Chesterfield is his cigarette."

Here's one more smoke story: Halsey Hall was a colorful radio announcer for the Twins. During a broadcast, Hall's cigar burned his sports jacket. His partners put out the blaze, but Hall's jacket was ruined. Minnesota catcher Jerry Zimmerman made this comment: "It's the only time in history that a sports jacket became a blazer."

ORIGINALLY PRINTED JULY 3, 2006.

Pudge a lock for Hall, but as a Tiger?

One of America's favorite weekends takes place at Cooperstown, N.Y., reaching a climax with the Hall of Fame induction.

Tigers fans might ask: Will any of the current Tigers reach the Hall of Fame? Detroit's last inductee — in 2000 — was manager Sparky Anderson, who chose to be designated as a Cincinnati Red. My candidate from the current team is Ivan Rodriguez.

Pudge is a cinch. The only question: Will he enter the Hall as a Tiger?

Pudge played 12 years for the Texas Rangers, one for the Florida Marlins. He was a member of the 2003 Marlins that won the World Series.

It would be a longshot for Rodriguez to enter the Hall as a Tiger. He would have to play in Detroit several more years. Otherwise, he'll wear a Rangers cap on his Hall plaque.

For the past few years, Tigers fans have rooted unsuccessfully for the Hall of Fame to induct right-hander Jack Morris, shortstop Alan Trammell and second baseman Lou Whitaker, but none has received enough votes. Now, hope rests on Rodriguez. He is the only possibility, unless another current Tiger can build a Hall-worthy career.

The 2006 major league inductee was pitcher

Bruce Sutter, along with 17 special electees from the Negro Leagues and pre-Negro eras.

Sutter is worthy of selection. Master of the split-finger fastball, he rode to fame on that newfangled pitch. After two starts in the minors, Bruce suffered an arm injury that threatened his career. He learned the splitter from Fred Martin, roving pitcher instructor with the Cubs.

With his new pitch, Sutter built a 12-year career, finishing with 300 saves and a 2.83 ERA. The six-time All-Star right-hander was the first to reach 200 and 300 saves.

I always had identified Sutter as a Cub, but his Hall plaque will have his likeness wearing a St. Louis Cardinals cap. He pitched five years in Chicago, four in St. Louis and three in Atlanta. His only World Series came in 1982, posting a win and two saves for the Cardinals in their seven-game victory over the Milwaukee Brewers.

Those to be honored with Sutter were elected by a committee of 12 Negro League historians in February. On the list is the late Effa Manley, owner of the Newark Eagles. She becomes the first woman elected to the Hall of Fame.

A glaring omission from this group is Buck O'Neil, Negro League star for 18 years. He managed the Kansas City Monarchs to five pennants and was the first black major league coach. He did not make the list of inductees. What a shame!

ORIGINALLY PRINTED JULY 24, 2006.

Replacements can become future stars

The Tigers' primary question mark in 2007 is the effect of Kenny Rogers' injury on their pennant chase. Will some other pitcher — Chad Durbin, perhaps — step in and have an outstanding year? Or will the Tigers be unable to fill the void for the first half of the season?

Stories of replacements going on to stardom are numerous. The most famous is how Wally Pipp's headache launched Lou Gehrig's Iron Man streak. Also, there's the less-known Bobby Thomson-Hank Aaron saga.

In February 1954, the Milwaukee Brewers obtained Thomson from the Giants to play leftfield. However, he suffered a broken leg during spring training, and Aaron — an infielder slated for the minors — replaced him.

Aaron turned in a fine rookie season, hitting .282 with 13 homers and 69 RBIs. But he suffered a broken leg that September, ending his season after 122 games but keeping him from serving in the military and thereby missing several seasons.

The Tigers had a Hall of Famer who broke into the lineup because of a veteran's misfortune. Charlie Gehringer got his shot at second base in 1926 when measles benched Frank O'Rourke.

More recently, there's the story of two Tigers

FREE PRESS FILE PHOTO

Jack Morris, who won 198 games as a Tiger, once was booed when named an injury replacement starter for Mark Fidrych in 1978.

pitchers, Mark (The Bird) Fidrych and Jack Morris. After Fidrych's brilliant 1976 rookie season, he struggled with injuries, never regaining his glory. Yet, he kept his crowd appeal, packing the park with each start.

Meanwhile, Morris made his debut with the Tigers in July 1977, but arm troubles sent him to the minors. He was back with the team in 1978, confined to the bullpen. On Saturday afternoon, April 22, Morris was a surprise starter against Texas.

Just minutes before the game, pitching coach Fred Gladding told Jack, "Fidrych's arm is hurting. He can't pitch. You're starting. Get ready."

"I'd been kidding around in the bullpen when I

got the news," Morris recalled. "I warmed up quickly. As I left the bullpen, I heard the PA announcer tell the big crowd, 'Ladies and gentlemen, Mark Fidrych, the Tigers' scheduled starter, will not pitch tonight. He is injured. The Tiger pitcher will be Jack Morris.' Walking toward the mound, I get a standing boo."

Morris pitched into the fifth inning and left with the Rangers leading, 3-0. The Tigers won, 7-6, in 10 innings. Jack broke into the regular rotation the following year. He won 17 and lost seven. For 12 of the next 13 seasons, he led the Tigers in wins. He was baseball's dominant pitcher in the 1980s and appeared in five All-Star Games and three World Series. In the 1991 Fall Classic, he was the MVP. That series, he pitched a masterpiece for the Twins, beating the Braves and John Smoltz, 1-0, in 10 innings.

After the funeral of Twins announcer Herb Carneal, I rode to the airport with Hall of Fame slugger Harmon Killebrew. "I can't understand why Morris isn't in the Hall of Fame," Harmon said. "He was the best pitcher in the '80s and brilliant in the World Series."

And, remember, Jack had to overcome replacing The Bird and getting — as he put it — a "standing boo."

ORIGINALLY PRINTED APRIL 16, 2007.

Thompson third to break color line

The media zeroes in on Jackie Robinson, emphasizing that he was the right choice to break baseball's color line.

What about the player who was the wrong choice to break the color line?

His name was Hank Thompson.

When I was a broadcaster for the New York Giants in the 1950s, Thompson, the team's third baseman, was enjoying the high point of a checkered career. I remember him as personable and popular with his teammates. We called him Snuffy, because of his habit of constantly sniffing. Hank played in two World Series (1951 and 1954) during eight seasons with the Giants.

Thompson's story was one of those "might have been" sagas. Gerry Fraley did a great job of depicting Hank's story recently in the St. Louis Post-Dispatch. Fraley noted that Thompson was the third man to break the color line, following Robinson and Larry Doby. Being third in any historical event only earns you a ticket to oblivion.

Thompson broke in with the St. Louis Browns in July 1947. The reception from his teammates was icy. They refused to participate in pregame practice with Hank and another black recruit, Willard Brown. Manager Muddy Ruel would not bother to discuss the newcomers. After five weeks, the Browns released both players.

Thompson returned to the Negro Leagues and then played in Cuba. The Giants spotted him there and he joined them July 15, 1949, becoming the only player to integrate two major league teams.

After the Giants released him following the 1956 season, Thompson quit baseball at the age of 31. From then on, his life went downhill. Always a heavy drinker, he drifted from job to job. He suffered through a divorce. Earlier, Thompson had served time in prison and even shot a man in a Dallas bar. He returned to his old ways and was charged with assault, theft and armed robbery. After serving four years of a 10-year prison sentence, he was paroled. Then he remarried and found a job.

Life was finally getting better for Thompson. After years of being without a wife, kids or a job, he finally had conquered his demons. But his good times didn't last. In September 1969, he suffered a heart attack and died at 43. On his headstone in Fresno, Calif., there is no mention of his baseball career, or that he was the third player to break the color line.

ORIGINALLY PRINTED APRIL 23, 2007.

Some ballyard yarns too good to be true

Some stories are too good to be true. Those yarns about Yogi Berra and his quotations, for instance. Yogi said some of them, but others are inventions of writers with overactive imaginations.

Former Tiger Germany Schaefer was the Yogi Berra of the early 1900s. He was a great comedian, but the authenticity of some of his feats is suspect.

I read an article about Schaefer and Tigers teammate Charley O'Leary in a 1954 Sporting News booklet written by John Drohan, a Boston sports writer. According to Drohan, Schaefer and O'Leary were friends with a young inventor they called Crazy Hank.

Crazy Hank, so the story goes, often would drive the two Tigers to Bennett Park in his new horseless carriage. Once, he told the two about the great possibilities of the gasoline engine.

"If I had $2,500," he said, "I could start a company here, and everybody on Michigan Avenue could have a horseless carriage. You boys could invest with me and make a fortune."

O'Leary said years later, "Germany and I were going to invest in a gold mine out West. We told Crazy Hank not to bother picking us up anymore and taking us to Bennett field. We were moving downtown to a hotel. Right after that, a fellow who had been a bookkeeper in Detroit heard about (Crazy Hank's) proposition and became Hank's partner. The bookkeeper became mayor of Detroit and later a United States senator from Michigan. His investment with Hank brought him $40 million. The bookkeeper was James Couzens.

"The gold mine we invested in turned out to be just a hole in the ground. We were the crazy guys — not Crazy Hank, whose real name was Henry Ford."

I checked Drohan's story with Bob Casey of Ford, an expert on the auto company's history. He could find no verification for it. Another automobile historian, Mark Patrick of the Detroit Public Library, researched it with his usual thoroughness and came up empty.

Finally, I phoned the Baseball Hall of Fame, and Freddy Berowski assured me there was nothing in Cooperstown to substantiate the article.

I have to conclude that it's just one more story that's too good to be true.

ORIGINALLY PRINTED JUNE 4, 2007.

A record Hall turnout in 2007

When Cal Ripken Jr. and Tony Gwynn entered the Baseball Hall of Fame in 2007, they attracted the largest crowd in the history of the event — an estimated 75,000.

This figure surpasses the 50,000 turnout in 1999 when Nolan Ryan, George Brett, Robin Yount and Orlando Cepeda entered the Hall. The third-largest crowd was the 40,000 — most of them Phillies fans — who attended the induction of Mike Schmidt and Richie Ashburn in 1995.

Certainly the Hall of Fame ceremonies have grown in stature.

Here are some random notes about the event and the shrine in Cooperstown:

Do you know the Hall of Famer who struck out in his only major league at-bat? It's Walter Alston. He reached the Hall not for his hitting ability, but for his record as manager of the Los Angeles Dodgers.

The first Tiger to make the Hall of Fame was — no surprise — Ty Cobb. He was elected in the first class of honorees in 1936. Cobb led the voting, garnering 98.23% of the ballots. That amount has since been eclipsed by Tom Seaver, Ryan and Ripken. Seaver achieved 98.84% in the 1992 elections.

Michigan is well-represented in the upper echelon. Hall of Fame president Dale Petroskey, a

Michigan State grad, was once a junior usher at Briggs Stadium. Senior vice president Bill Haase was a top Tiger executive for many years.

One of the strangest induction years was 1948. Herb Pennock and Pie Traynor were the electees. However, Pennock died before the ceremony. Traynor was there, but the festivities were postponed because his plaque had not been delivered. Traynor had to wait until the next year to receive his plaque.

ORIGINALLY PRINTED JULY 23, 2007.

Leyland: Baseball's Shakespeare

Ever since Jim Leyland began his successful stint as Tigers manager, a lot of folks have analyzed him.

Now, he is even being compared to William Shakespeare. This observation comes from Martha Baldoni of Perrysburg, Ohio. Martha's husband, the late Dr. Louis Baldoni, was the family doctor for the Leylands.

"I've recognized Jim's flair for drama, and the similarity of his language to Shakespeare's. So, I thought of writing a comparison of the two," she wrote me.

Here is Martha's analysis:

Director Leyland, who has spent four decades in baseball, defines his world in a few careful words, "We are entertainers."

Shakespeare wrote: "All the world's a stage, and all the men and women merely players."

Leyland, whose magic conjured the Tigers into a Cinderella story in 2006, credits what he calls stuff — the talent each player brings to the game.

Prospero, who possessed great magical powers in "The Tempest," said, "We are such stuff as dreams are made on and our little life is rounded with a sleep."

When fans booed a Sean Casey fielding error,

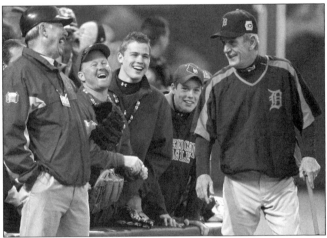

JULIAN H. GONZALEZ

Jim Leyland, who led the Tigers to the 2006 World Series, is one of only seven managers to win both AL and NL pennants.

Leyland, who took personal offense at their behavior, observed that their action "proves they don't know much about baseball."

Shakespeare was no more graphic when in "As You Like It," Lord Amiens says, "Blow, blow thou winter wind. Thou are not so unkind as man's ingratitude."

Leyland continues to tell his Tigers, "Act like swaggering champions."

In "Measure For Measure," Shakespeare wrote, "Our doubts are traitors, and make us lose the good we oft might win, by fearing to attempt."

Leyland admitted that "the Yankees might intimidate one of his rookie pitchers." But in a different era, Achilles from "Troilus and Cressida" expressed the same emotion: "My mind is troubled, like a fountain stirred. And I myself see not the bottom of it."

When his players grow weary, Leyland encourages them to "pick it up." This is close to King Henry V's version, "Once more unto the breach, dear friends, once more."

And Jim's "All I ask is that you play all nine innings" echoes the classic advice Polonius gave Laertes: "This above all, to thine own self be true. And it must follow as the night the day. Thou canst not then be false to any man."

In his postgame news conference, Leyland often paraphrases Shakespeare's observation in "Henry VIII": " 'Tis ten to one this play can never please all that are here."

Finally, as the Tigers' season rolls along, Jim and Shakespeare are thinking alike. Leyland has said, "Last year is in the book. This year is not in the book." The 16th Century bard's Ophelia put it this way: "Lord, we know what we are, but know not what we may be."

ORIGINALLY PRINTED JULY 30, 2007.

ON THE AIR

 ERNIE ON HIS START AS A SPORTS ANNOUNCER:
I think the idea was instead of writing it, I was talking it. And I had really trained myself to be a sports writer, so my background maybe helped me a little bit. And they didn't mind my voice too much. **99**

DISC 1, ERNIE HARWELL'S AUDIO SCRAPBOOK

Celebs secondary to the game

've said it before, but I want to say it again for emphasis. I never liked putting celebrities on the air during a baseball broadcast.

To me, the game is always first. Trying to interview someone over the play-by-play is a distraction.

My ultimate test for this credo came when the Tigers opened the 1999 season against the Texas Rangers at The Ballpark in Arlington. George W. Bush, then governor of Texas, was beginning his campaign for president. As the game progressed, his staff was escorting him through the stadium and eventually to the press box, and the radio and TV booths.

I had known Mr. Bush for several years — first when he was owner of the Rangers and later when he was governor. When he was an owner, he often dropped by our booth to chat about the team and baseball in general. I was very fond of him and respected his knowledge of baseball.

It was the middle of the seventh inning when Gov. Bush and his entourage reached our booth the night of that opener. With the mike off, I turned around and greeted him. We had about 30 seconds of friendly conversation.

Gov. Bush had gone on the air with the other TV and radio guys. Now it was my turn with him. But the Tigers were taking the field for the last of the seventh.

Brian Moehler had no-hit the Rangers for six innings. The drama of a potential no-hitter was beginning to build.

"It was good to see you, Governor. Please visit us again," I said to Mr. Bush. I then turned and focused my concentration on the game.

The Bush entourage moved to another booth to resume on-the-air interviews. The last of the seventh inning began. After Moehler had retired a batter, Juan Gonzalez singled to break up the no-hitter.

It didn't seem to matter to Bush's career that I had not interviewed him that spring night in Texas. He went on to take his place in history as our 43rd president.

And if I ever have a chance to remind him of that opener, he might even agree with my credo that the game always comes first.

ORIGINALLY PRINTED MAY 3, 2004.

Griffey's 500th called in classy way

When a radio or television play-by-play announcer approaches a historic event, he can broadcast it one of two ways: He can work weeks ahead preparing an apt phrase he hopes will remain forever in the recollection of his listeners; or he can accept the big event as part of the game and react in a natural way.

My preference always has been to respond as the moment dictates — no overpreparation, no overanticipation. Just count on your spontaneity.

On Father's Day 2004, the voices of the Cincinnati Reds — Marty Brennaman on radio and George Grande on television — called Ken Griffey Jr.'s 500th home run just the way I like it.

On radio, Brennaman said: "The pitch. And a high drive, hit back into deep rightfield. Junior has just knocked the door down to the 500 club. A high drive into the lower deck in right. No. 30 touches 'em all. Boy, what a Father's Day gift for Senior."

Grande put it this way: "The wait is over, folks. Junior, take a deep breath and enjoy it. That's 500, and that's your ticket to the Hall of Fame." Then, after a television shot of Ken Griffey Sr. and the family, Grande added: "What a Father's Day present for Senior and the whole family."

Brennaman told Kevin Kelly of the Cincinnati

Enquirer, "I just said whatever came to mind. The only thing you hope for is that whatever you say, it flows, and you don't stumble over your words, which I didn't."

Grande expressed the same approach to the 500th homer. "I've always felt that we announcers just go along for the ride," he said. "I like to let it go and play it as it goes."

There is a sidelight to this story. Weeks before the home run, Griffey had requested that on the radio, either Brennaman or partner Joe Nuxhall call the historic blow. His request would take first-year announcer Steve Stewart off the broadcast and substitute one of the veterans. I did not approve of this intrusion. I believe that whoever is on the air when the big event is about to occur should stay there. The game is always bigger than an announcer.

When players dictate broadcast procedure, we don't know where their interference might take us.

Brennaman handled the pressure of the situation with class, but the Griffey proposal became academic because the home run came during one of Marty's innings (the sixth).

With Grande on television, there was no issue. He always handled all the play-by-play, with his partner Chris Welsh serving as color man.

Marty and George were tops. They broadcast the big event in true style.

ORIGINALLY PRINTED JUNE 28, 2004.

All dream jobs have possible nightmares

Do people in one certain profession have a common nightmare? I think they do in baseball broadcasting. You might be surprised to learn that the most prevalent nightmare among broadcasters is not making a huge mistake in a World Series or playoff game. Or even cursing on the air or allowing profanity to slip into your presentation. It's not any one of those that would seem to be an odds-on favorite in the bad-dream league.

I discovered over the years that my dreams always centered on getting to the ballpark. Sometimes I'd be late. Other times I would have an accident on the expressway. Or maybe after I had reached the park, I wouldn't be able to get to the booth. That was the most frustrating. And it was the specific nightmare that haunted me the most. I'd find a gate and couldn't get in. Maybe the attendant kept me out. I wouldn't have my credentials, or sometimes no one would be at the gate and it would be locked. I'd circle the park, never able to get in. When I awoke, I'd still feel frustrated.

When I was a working broadcaster, I often discussed nightmares with other broadcasters. "I have that same dream," they would tell me. "I have it over and over. It's about the only kind of dream I have."

There must be some kind of psychological explanation for this recurring event. Is there a deepseated fear in all of us about losing our jobs? Or do we all eat too much dream-inducing junk food too close to bedtime? Or are all of us just goofy?

And what about other professions? Does the surgeon have nightmares about his scalpel slipping and cutting the wrong organ? Does the lawyer dream about forgetting his closing remarks to the jury? Does fear of laryngitis haunt every singer, actor and minister?

How about baseball players? Their nightmares might include striking out with the bases loaded or dropping a fly ball. But it's probably something else — something we fans might not even suspect.

Some day I'll ask some of my baseball-playing friends and find out what their dreams tell them they fear the most.

ORIGINALLY PRINTED JULY 26, 2004.

In booth, hobby was music to my ears

When I broadcast baseball play-by-play, I had two major hobbies — playing golf and writing music.

My partners and I always welcomed anyone connected with either endeavor into our radio booth. Sometimes our visitors went on the air with us. More often, they simply enjoyed watching the games.

We'd usually play golf in the morning — at home or on the road — and then the pro, groundskeeper or caddie master would be our guest at the game that night. With the music folks, it was the other way around. They'd visit us in the afternoon, and we'd enjoy their performance that evening.

I'd always keep my music in the booth, just in case some recording artist showed up. In the mid-'60s this led to my first record on a major label.

In those days, George Toles was a DJ on WJBK Radio. His guests one morning were Homer and Jethro, the duo famous for their novelty songs on the RCA label.

"Jethro and I are avid baseball fans," Homer told Toles after the interview. "Could you help us get tickets for the Tigers' game?"

"I can do better than that," Toles told him. "I'll get you two seats in the radio booth. Ernie Harwell would love to have you as his guests."

So the musical duo sat in with Ray Lane and me. Between innings, I pulled out one of my songs, "Upside Down," and showed it to them. After the game, they thanked us, and then Jethro turned to me and said, "We will put your song on our next album."

I never heard from them again. But sometime in November the mailman brought an RCA album called "Something Stupid" by Homer and Jethro. Sure enough, it included "Upside Down."

The liner notes said: "Detroit Tiger baseball announcer wrote this one, and we think it's a fine observation of the world today, as seen from the press box at Tiger Stadium. We were up there with Ernie one day, and from there the world looks upside down. In fact, the Mets were on top in the National League."

Since then, 65 more of my songs have been recorded by various artists. Needless to say, I have more no-hitters than Nolan Ryan.

One more note about music. In our booth I always left my songs and a shabby overcoat. Once, when the Tigers were on the road, somebody broke into our booth and stole everything except the overcoat and my music.

Does that tell you what folks thought about my music?

ORIGINALLY PRINTED MAY 31, 2005.

Catchy phrases come naturally

Some of baseball's best broadcasters have signature phrases. Other top-notch announcers play it straight.

I don't think it matters. I've always advised young broadcasters not to sit down and contrive a phrase. If it happens, so be it. But let it come naturally.

I'm sure the great Yankees announcer Mel Allen came upon his "How about that?" without working on it in his study. I remember the first time I heard him use that phrase. It was in the early '50s when I was a New York Giants broadcaster. I had announced a day game at the Polo Grounds and then gone home to hear Mel's Yankees broadcast from Cleveland. New York had a huge lead (something like 14-2) when Larry Doby of the Indians was thrown out trying to steal home. Not able to believe Doby's gaffe, Mel kept saying, "How about that?" over and over. Another Allen signature phrase was his home run call, "Going, going, gone." I don't think Mel realized this phrase had been used for the first time eight years before he started broadcasting. Its originator was Harry Hartman, announcer of Cincinnati games in the early days of radio.

One of the best home run calls belonged to the pioneer broadcaster Rosey Roswell, who worked for the Pirates in the early '30s. When Rosey's beloved Bucs were on the road, he didn't travel with them, but did re-creations from the studio. Rosey invented an Aunt Minnie who lived near the ballpark. He would describe the flight of a home run and then top it off with "Open the window, Aunt Minnie, here it comes." Aunt Minnie never opened the window in time, and Rosey would smash a pane of glass in the studio to give his listeners the feeling of a homer crashing through the old aunt's window.

Let's not overlook "Holy Cow." Several broadcasters made this one their signature phrase. I can recall at least three — Harry Caray, Phil Rizzuto and Earl Gillespie. Caray and Rizzuto feuded for years over who originated that phrase. Gillespie, who broadcast for the first major league Milwaukee team, sat aside and let them fight it out.

My opinion is that "Holy Cow" was first used by a monk in Tibet many centuries before Phil, Harry or Earl made the scene.

ORIGINALLY PRINTED JUNE 27, 2005.

Booth visit worked well with Kell

Allowing visitors in the booth always has been a problem for broadcasters. You have to deal with sponsors, celebrities and fans who want to watch the game from the perch.

Visitors never bothered me. I concentrated on the game, and a jammed booth was OK. However, many announcers disliked having anyone in the booth except the regular crew.

Putting visitors on the air was a different matter — something I never wanted to do. Sometimes you had no choice. The sponsor insisted on a celebrity appearing to plug a show or a book. Or the team's public relations director would drag along the Peach Queen or the mayor.

When I broadcast Atlanta Crackers games in the Southern League, I asked an injured Atlanta pitcher named Earl McGowan to do some play-by-play. He had just taken over the mike when a Crackers batter hit a foul to leftfield.

"There's a foul ball headed for the _____ bleachers," he shouted, using the N-word to describe the stands. African-American fans bombarded the club with letters of protest. Club president Earl Mann told me the next day, "Never again will you put one of my players on the air."

During the 1957 season in Baltimore, I put anoth-

FREE PRESS FILE PHOTO

George Kell, who visited with Ernie Harwell in the booth in 1957, made a smooth transition from star player to broadcaster.

er player on the air with a happier result. George Kell was in the final year of his playing career. Back and knee injuries had plagued him all season. Then he was beaned. While on the disabled list, he visited our booth. I introduced him to free food and drink in the pressroom and asked him to broadcast an inning.

Kell was a natural. He enjoyed his taste of broadcasting. After the season, he accepted an offer from CBS-TV to work on its "Game of the Week" pregame show. That brief exposure led Kell to a job with Van Patrick on Tigers broadcasts in 1959. Except for the 1964 season, Kell broadcast either Tigers radio or TV until his retirement after the 1996 season.

When Patrick left the Tigers after the 1959 season, Kell recommended that the Tigers hire me from Baltimore. I came for the 1960 season and was able to stay awhile.

When it comes to using visitors on the air, you win some and lose some.

ORIGINALLY PRINTED AUG. 22, 2005.

All-Star broadcast is the toughest

When they broadcast the 2006 All-Star Game, Joe Buck and Tim McCarver (TV) and Dan Shulman and Dave Campbell (radio) will face the baseball announcer's most difficult challenge. To work this game is a great honor, and these crews will turn in stellar performances, but the job is also the toughest in the business.

There are other daunting assignments. What about an early exhibition game when players you'll never see again make the lineup? Or a September snoozer with your team out of the pennant race and playing out the schedule?

I've stumbled through a lot of those spring and September turkeys, but I believe the All-Star Game is more of a challenge to the announcer.

The chief problem with the broadcast is the number of players on each squad. You know the guys from your own league, but many of the players representing the other league are strange to you. You've seen them only once in a while. Also, each manager feels compelled to play everyone on his roster. Lineup changes are fast and furious.

With so many players coming and going, you have little chance to give enough information or insight about any of them. Yet you must fully prepare yourself with facts about everybody, because you never know who might or might not play. The All-Star PR staff overwhelms you with information about each player, so it becomes a momentous task to select the facts you want to use on your broadcast.

Because the All-Star Game is more of a spectacle than a contest, it creates other challenges. With hundreds of media people swarming all over the ballpark, officials must establish new regulations to restrict access to the players. Personal contacts become lost in the shuffle of the crowd. Your broadcast likely will suffer without this personal touch.

There's another drawback in announcing the All-Star Game. This one looms larger on TV than on radio. Your director always establishes his own story line, and he insists that you follow it. This emphasis takes precedence over the game itself. You tweak your style to the director's story line, and sometimes you don't feel comfortable in your performance.

Don't get me wrong. I've always enjoyed working an All-Star classic, but I still think it's the toughest of all baseball games to broadcast.

ORIGINALLY PRINTED JULY 10, 2006.

Many ways to mispronounce

A challenge for any baseball announcer is to pronounce players' names correctly. And with the recent influx of foreign players, the challenge is greater.

Foreign names never bothered me as much as some American ones. For example, John Lowenstein or Mike Epstein. I could never remember whether the final sound was steen or stine.

The only way to find out about a player's name is to ask him. Guidelines in press books often are inaccurate. When the yearly American League Red Book was edited by PR director Bob Holbrook, phonetic spellings were tinged with Holbrook's Boston accent.

Ethnic groups dislike announcers anglicizing names. After Dick Tracewski joined the Tigers in 1966, I received several letters from Polish fans.

"You're mispronouncing Tracewski's name," they wrote. "You should call him Trazeffski."

Speaking of Polish names, when I broadcasted Baltimore Colts football in 1956, the Colt boosters staged a banquet. My partner, Chuck Thompson, attended, but I couldn't go. A fan told Chuck, "I don't like you guys mispronouncing the name of our center, Dick Szymanski. And tell that to your partner, Ernie Hardwel, too."

Another problem is a player who changes pronunciation in mid-career. In his rookie season of 1957, Washington first baseman Julio Becquer called himself "Becker." Three years later, he switched to a fancier "Beckaire."

Art Houtteman, who pitched for the Tigers in 1945-53, kept changing the first syllable of his last name back and forth from Hoo to How. I can't even remember the final verdict.

In the pre-radio days, not many fans knew how to pronounce difficult player names. There were only newspaper reports, so players such as Evers, Lajoie, Waddell and Cicotte could be said any way a fan chose.

More important for a player in those days was how his name fit into the daily box score. It was a problem that plagued young Remus native Antonio Bordetzki early in his career. A sports writer friend suggested Bordetzki change his name because it contained too many letters.

"What should I call myself?" the young player asked.

"It doesn't matter, as long as you're brief."

"All right," said Bordetzki, "I'll call myself Brief."

Antonio (Bunny) Brief played briefly in the big leagues with the St. Louis Browns, White Sox and Pirates, but is best remembered as one of the all-time outstanding hitters in American Association history.

Fans often misinterpret the announcers' comments. Doing New York Giants play-by-play, I once

Tiger Aurelio Rodriguez's mitt helped him win the 1976 AL Gold Glove at third base, ending Brooks Robinson's 16-year run.

tried to compliment Dodgers shortstop Pee Wee Reese, saying, "He plays shortstop like he spells his name — with a lot of ease."

The Brooklyn fans got mad. They thought I was saying E's for errors.

Then there was the case of Tigers third baseman Aurelio Rodriguez. A 9-year-old at a Tiger Stadium game said to his dad, "That Rodriguez doesn't look so old to me."

"What do you mean?" his dad asked.

"Well," the youngster answered, "Ernie Harwell is always calling him that really old Rodriguez."

ORIGINALLY PRINTED AUG. 21, 2006.

Chats with umps always a delight

The best part about broadcasting baseball was being around the ballpark. I always enjoyed my time before a game when I could chat with managers, coaches, players, trainers, writers, broadcasters and fans. But I think my favorite moments were those spent with the umpires.

I started that custom in 1946, the year I began announcing Atlanta Crackers games in the Southern League.

The Southern League had some colorful umpires. Harry (Steamboat) Johnson was the best known. He was called Steamboat because his booming calls had reminded Atlanta writer Ed Danforth of a steamboat whistle.

Atlanta was also where I first knew Nicholas (Red) Jones, who umpired in the American League and after retirement became a popular banquet speaker in Detroit.

When I reached the major leagues in 1948, I continued my visits with the umpires.

The umps always arrived an hour before the game. I'd sit with them and talk about many subjects. We'd discuss interpretations of rules, abilities of managers and players, and the problems of travel.

I met many of their families. It would usually be

a dad who came into the umpires' dressing room. Sometimes, the kids would be around.

Once in Cleveland, crew chief Jim Evans asked me to rub up the balls in preparation for the game that night.

Over the years, I stuck nicknames on some of the umpires. Mike Reilly was Cornflakes because he came from Battle Creek. I dubbed Joe Brinkman The Professor because he ran an umpire school in Florida. And Chuck Meriwether became the "maître d' from Tennessee" in reference to his winter job at a Nashville restaurant.

Umpires were great sources of information. Because they didn't represent any team, they were objective in their opinions about the quality of teams, players and managers.

I never stayed long in their dressing room. Sometimes, it was just a quick "hello." But I always made it a practice to be there before each game. They didn't get visits from many members of the media, and I really cherished my time with them.

One of the proudest moments of my career came when the umps presented me with a special trophy during my final year of broadcasting. It was just a simple ceremony in the privacy of their dressing room. Nobody else knew it was happening. But it was an event I will always remember.

ORIGINALLY PRINTED JUNE 11, 2007.

Re-creations sound live but weren't

There always has been a fascination among radio listeners about the re-created baseball game. I get more questions about this than any other phase of the broadcasting business.

In a re-creation, the announcer is not at the ballpark. He is live in a studio but gets play-by-play information from another source. It might be a telephone call or a telegraphic report.

I'm not sure anyone still does a re-creation, but when I started in radio in the 1940s, it was common. In 1948, broadcasters began to travel with their major league teams and re-creations gradually disappeared. The Pittsburgh Pirates were the last major league team to re-create, abandoning the practice in the early 1950s.

When I joined the Brooklyn Dodgers in 1948, they sent their announcers on the road for the first time in the last half of that season.

Even then, we did re-creations of other National League games from the WMGM studios in Manhattan, if the Dodgers had a day off or were rained out.

In a re-creation, the announcer was more actor than reporter. A telegrapher in the away city would send game details to another telegrapher in the studio. The studio telegrapher would type out the details. It would go this way: "Whitaker at bat. B1W.

FLOGS. Strike two called. B2H. Out, short to first."
The announcer would enhance that skeleton report, saying, "Lou Whitaker is up." He would describe Whitaker's stance and tell all about the defensive alignment. B1W would become ball one outside. FLOGS was foul over the grandstand, etc.

Once, former President Ronald Reagan invited a group of announcers and writers to the White House for lunch. He regaled us with stories of his days of re-creating White Sox and Cubs games. Reagan broadcasted those games over WHO in Des Moines, Iowa. He was never at a game — home or away.

He told us that once his telegraphic connection broke, and he filled the delay by having the Cubs batter foul off 16 straight pitches.

There were other tricks, too. If the wire broke down, you would have a dog run on the field. Or maybe a light sprinkle. Anything to keep talking. Generally, the announcer would stay about a half inning behind the action in case something went wrong. But if he wanted to leave the studio right after the game, he would have each batter in the final inning hit the first pitch.

Some broadcasters did a better re-creation than a live game, because the facts were written out for them ahead of time in contrast to reacting to a play on the field.

I enjoyed re-creations, but broadcasting directly from the park was much better radio and a lot more fun.

ORIGINALLY PRINTED JULY 2, 2007.

TALES OF THE TIGERS

ERNIE ON THE 1968 TIGERS CHAMPIONSHIP:

    It was a great factor in the healing of the city because people could root for a black guy or a white guy or a purple guy or a green guy or whatever ... if he was a Tiger. And they all forgot about the other stuff.

DISC 3, ERNIE HARWELL'S AUDIO SCRAPBOOK

Bergman at bat: A homer to remember

Now that the Pistons have brought Detroit another NBA title, what will be the defining photographic symbol of that championship? Will it be Chauncey Billups celebrating with his NBA Finals MVP trophy or another classic shot?

In the Tigers' memory book, the 1968 champs are represented by the photo of Mickey Lolich jumping into the arms of Bill Freehan, after Bill had caught Tim McCarver's pop foul for the final out of the World Series in St. Louis.

Even more vivid is the famous Mary Schroeder picture that symbolized the 1984 Series championship. That one is the best-selling Free Press poster — Kirk Gibson's dramatic celebration of his home run in the fifth and deciding game.

That '84 team had many more highlights than Gibby's homer. You could point to the team's 35-5 start. Also Jack Morris' no-hitter, Chet Lemon's catches, Alan Trammell's World Series MVP performance and Willie Hernandez's great bullpen work.

My favorite moment didn't turn the season around and wasn't a pivotal World Series play. Instead, it was one of the best at-bats I ever saw in my broadcasting career — Dave Bergman batting against Roy Lee Jackson of Toronto in a June 4 game at Tiger Stadium.

The game was tied at 3 when Bergman batted in the 10th inning. There were two runners on base and two outs. After the count reached 3-2, Dave fouled off seven pitches, then hit Jackson's 13th pitch into the rightfield seats for a 6-3 victory.

It was Bergman's first home run of the season and the most dramatic of the seven he hit that year. That seven-minute at-bat highlighted ABC's first Monday telecast of the season and became a signature for Dave's career. It was a classic example of Bergman's dedication and tenacity.

ORIGINALLY PRINTED JUNE 21, 2004.

With all due respect, Tram manages media

Now that the Tigers' 2004 season is over and report cards are being distributed, I submit a grade for manager Alan Trammell in a rarely regarded category. For his performance in media relations, he earns an A.

I realize this phase of Tram's job doesn't overly excite the average fan. Yet, it's very important to Alan from both the standpoint of his career and team harmony.

From his first news conference after his appointment as manager through his first two seasons, Tram has excelled in the way he has handled himself. All media members are treated alike — with friendliness and courtesy. Tram goes out of his way to accommodate. He is honest in his comments but never denigrates his players.

When he shows this kind of respect in his media dealings, his attitude is reflected by his team. It's proverbial that players on a major league team emulate their leader. Soon media members from other cities also begin to realize that the Tigers will be friendly, polite and respectful.

So, Tram, take your report card home, get it signed and bring it back to me.

ORIGINALLY PRINTED OCT. 4, 2004.

All-Star memories: Bring your uniform

t's about time Detroit hosted another All-Star Game. Until 2005, all the original franchises except the Tigers had been awarded the game at least four times. It's not surprising that New York (often with three clubs in the city) and the original site, Chicago in 1933, are tied for the most with seven apiece.

The 1951 All-Star Game at Detroit originally was scheduled for Philadelphia but was switched because Detroit was celebrating its 250th birthday. The only other switch came in 1953. The Boston Braves had been chosen to host the game, but the franchise moved to Milwaukee, so the game was played in Cincinnati's Crosley Field.

Ty Cobb, the greatest Tiger of all, never played in an All-Star Game. His career ended in 1928, five years before the game was established. The closest Cobb came to All-Star action was when he threw out the first ball at Detroit's 1951 game.

Another Tigers great, Harry Heilmann, died on the eve of that game and was honored with a silent tribute in pregame ceremonies at Briggs Stadium, later known as Tiger Stadium. When Heilmann was near death, Cobb visited him at his hospital bed and whispered to Heilmann that he had been elected to the Hall of Fame.

Cobb's gesture was a lie. The vote hadn't been taken. Heilmann was inducted into Cooperstown in 1952.

The Tigers were well represented in other All-Star lore. Charlie Gehringer, Detroit's only All-Star in 1933, still holds the record for highest batting average (.500) among players with 20 or more at-bats. Although he had 110 RBIs at the break in 1935, Hank Greenberg was left off the American League team by his own manager, Mickey Cochrane.

Al Kaline remains the youngest position player to start an All-Star Game. Kaline was 20 years, 6 months and 23 days old when he suited up for the 1955 game at Milwaukee's County Stadium. He appeared in more games (16) than any other Tiger. That is eight short of the All-Star record of 24, shared by Hank Aaron, Willie Mays and Stan Musial. Musial and Mays appeared 24 straight years.

Two other Tigers records relating to the All-Star Game never made the record book: Most times left at an airport after an All-Star Game, one — held by Mickey Lolich. Denny McLain reneged on his promise to fly Lolich back to Detroit after the 1969 game at RFK Stadium in Washington. Most times reporting without a uniform — Lou Whitaker. His oversight necessitated a shopping trip for a store-bought uniform to wear at the Metrodome in Minneapolis in 1985.

ORIGINALLY PRINTED JULY 11, 2005.

Martin's hat trick was a winner

Billy Martin's famous hat trick in 1972 was a unique event in Tigers history. That was the day Detroit broke a losing streak with a lineup picked out of the manager's cap.

The Tigers had lost four straight and 10 of 13, dropping from first place to second in the American League East.

Martin — always full of surprises — entered the Tiger Stadium clubhouse and said, "All right, guys, today we do it different. The batting order is in my cap. You pick a slip of paper, and that's your place in the lineup."

"Is he nuts?" said Jim Northrup. "I can't believe this is happening. What's coming next?"

Cap in hand, Martin walked around the room, and the players picked their slips.

Norman Cash drew the leadoff spot.

"Guess I'll have to wear my fast shoes," he said.

"Don't worry about it," John Hiller shouted from a nearby corner. "Those shoes ain't any faster than you are."

Other players dug into the cap and picked their positions in the batting order. Ed Brinkman, who hit .203 that season, selected the cleanup spot. "About time I hit fourth," Brinkman said before ducking back slaps and elbow jabs from teammates.

It was a Sunday doubleheader against Cleveland. The Indians pitched their ace, 18-game winner Gaylord Perry, in the opener.

Martin's cap trick worked. The Tigers won, 3-2.

The hero? New cleanup man Brinkman. With the Tigers trailing, 2-1, in the sixth inning, Brinkman doubled in Willie Horton with the tying run, then scored the winner on Tony Taylor's single.

Between games, Martin beamed as he accepted credit for the slump-breaking victory. "I didn't realize I had such a smart hat," he told Free Press writer Jim Hawkins.

HAT'S ALL, FOLKS

The batting order in Game 1 on Aug. 13, 1972:

1. Norm Cash, 1B.
2. Jim Northrup, RF.
3. Willie Horton, LF.
4. Ed Brinkman, SS.
5. Tony Taylor, 2B.
6. Duke Sims, C.
7. Mickey Stanley, CF.
8. Aurelio Rodriguez, 3B.
9. Woodie Fryman, P.

The euphoria faded in the second game. Billy returned to his traditional batting order, and Cleveland beat the Tigers, 9-2, coasting to victory with a five-run fifth inning.

The Tigers bounced back and won the East Division. The Tigers lost to Oakland in the playoffs in five games.

But to me, 1972 always will be the year of Martin's hat trick.

ORIGINALLY PRINTED AUG. 8, 2005.

Tigers' fireman Hiller a true survivor

Here's unsolicited advice to Tigers uniformed personnel trying to survive after the season: Study the John Hiller Guide to Baseball Survival.

If anybody could write such a book, it's Hiller. Despite three heart attacks early in his career, he became the best relief pitcher in Tigers history. Even in retirement, he continues to be a survivor. In the summer of 2005, another leg amputation threatened Hiller. But a visit to Henry Ford Hospital assured him he had triumphed again.

"The doctor told me not to worry about the numbness and soreness," Hiller said from his Iron Mountain home. "It's a part of the aging process. Again, I've dodged amputation."

Hiller's heart scare early in his 15-year Tigers career was more of a threat. He was 27 in January 1971, when he suffered three heart attacks at his Duluth, Minn., home. After five weeks in the hospital, John heard his doctor say, "Look for another job. You'll never pitch again."

Instead of the usual cardiac surgery, John underwent an intestinal bypass. By November 1971, he had quit drinking and smoking and was going through strenuous rehab, vowing to defy the experts.

After three heart attacks in 1971, Tigers reliever John Hiller
vowed to return to baseball. In 1973, he set a record for saves (38)
and was named AL comeback player of the year.

Heart specialists refused to clear him to pitch.
General manager Jim Campbell finally budged. He
said, "We don't want you dying on the mound. We'll
sign you as a batting practice pitcher but reduce
your salary from $20,000 to $17,000."

Hiller agreed. Meanwhile, he found an advocate
in the internationally famous Dr. William Hurst.
"Let him pitch," Hurst told the Tigers.

Hiller's test came at Chicago on July 8, 1972.
Manager Billy Martin took left-hander Les Cain
and Hiller to the bullpen before a night game.

"Warm up," he said. "I'll keep one of you and release the other."

Said Hiller: "Cain was a good pitcher, but after all I'd gone through, no man — I don't care who — was going to be better than me that day."

He survived.

Although Hiller had not faced a batter in a year and a half, he relieved that night for three innings. The White Sox beat the Tigers, but Hiller realized he had finished the long, hard journey back. That's what really counted.

Hiller became the Tigers' greatest reliever. The next season, he notched 38 saves and was named comeback player of the year in the American League. In '74 he won 17 games in relief and made the All-Star team.

Several years after retiring, Hiller returned to the Tigers as a roving pitching coach. But a circulatory blockage behind his knee ended his comeback. A Lakeland surgeon told John his leg must be amputated.

"No way," Hiller told him and immediately returned to the Upper Peninsula, where he and his wife, Lynette, live year-round.

Hiller goes to Lakeland each spring for Tigers fantasy camp, but he likes the challenge of surviving our winters.

He has taught all of us how to survive.

ORIGINALLY PRINTED SEPT. 19, 2005.

Old friend Leyland back home

So long, Alan Trammell. Hello, Jim Leyland. That's the way we start the Tigers' 2006 season. I'll miss Tram. There has never been a classier guy in baseball. But Leyland is an excellent choice to succeed him. I've known Leyland for a long time and I — like most folks in baseball — hold him in high regard.

There's not a lot new I can tell you about Leyland. He comes to us with a fine resume. The writers in spring training have devoted a great deal of print to him. During the season, they will examine him more. But I do have a few observations about the new guy.

He is honest and straightforward. No frills about Leyland. He won't hesitate to speak his mind to one of his players — or to anybody else. But he is not a tyrant. He is a man with feelings. He can put himself in the other guy's situation and is very understanding.

Leyland is a leader who knows how to organize his team and direct it with authority. He is a baseball man through and through. He has special respect for the game — a quality I deeply admire.

I first heard about Leyland when he managed at Evansville, Ind., then a Tigers' Triple-A club. I had met him previously at various spring trainings but had no close association with him until seeing him at Evansville.

During the baseball strike of 1981, Paul Carey and I had no major league games to broadcast. WJR Radio sent us to Evansville to broadcast Triplets games. We enjoyed those games, and we enjoyed getting to know Leyland. You could tell his players liked him and wanted to play hard for him.

Jim's earlier minor league managerial success had made him a favorite to someday manage the Tigers. But Jim Campbell bypassed Leyland in 1979 when he replaced Les Moss with Sparky Anderson. After winning the division title at Evansville in 1981, Leyland had to take another route to become a major league manager. His accomplishments at Pittsburgh and Florida vindicated the confidence Carey and I had in him.

Now, Leyland has returned to manage in the majors. I think Tigers fans will learn to appreciate him.

ORIGINALLY PRINTED APRIL 3, 2006.

Music man armed with talent

In his latest song, Bill Slayback describes the fulfillment of every player's dream — the big leagues. Bill, who pitched for the Tigers in 1972-74, had one of baseball's most hectic but brilliant debuts. His career was meteoric — from a dazzling start to a sore arm. I remember him best as a loyal friend, a cowriter of songs and the most versatile major leaguer I ever knew.

Not only is Slayback a songwriter, he is a professional photographer, a skilled portrait painter and an illustrator. Bill can sing and play any musical instrument. He toured with Jose Feliciano. He is a recording artist for several well-known labels. Also, he has constructed his own sound studio, has built his own furniture and has done commercials for Nike, Budweiser, "Days of Our Lives" and ABC.

His playing career might have been as brilliant as his versatile off-field success if manager Billy Martin had not misused him his first season.

Slayback started in the Tigers' farm system at 21. In his second minor league season, 1969, he moved from Batavia to Lakeland midseason. A veteran player-coach named Jim Leyland caught Bill's first Lakeland game in Tampa. In 1972, Bill joined the Tigers.

"I was pitching for Toledo," he said. "We were in Charleston when Billy Martin phoned and told me to get to Tiger Stadium right away. I flew to Toledo, then drove to Detroit."

After reaching the city, Slayback couldn't find Tiger Stadium. It was 3 p.m., and he was getting desperate. He stopped at a service station.

"When I asked the workers for directions, they noticed my California tag," he said. "They asked me my name. Then they said I was pitching that night and showed me the stadium, just a few blocks away."

Slayback started that evening, June 26, against the Yankees. He no-hit the Yankees for seven innings before Johnny Callison led off the eighth with a single. Slayback allowed three more hits and didn't finish the game, but he notched a 4-3 win.

Bill's success continued. He pitched three straight complete-game victories before the All-Star break, fanning 29. In one game, he struck out Texas slugger Frank Howard four times on 12 pitches. When Howard joined the Tigers later that season, he presented his strikeout bat to Bill.

Then it fell apart for Slayback. After the brilliant start, Martin pitched him in relief with two days' rest. His young arm couldn't take the punishment. He finished the year 5-6 with a 3.20 ERA.

By next season, Bill's arm still hadn't responded. He pitched only two innings for the Tigers. Ralph Houk took over as manager in 1974, but Slayback's arm was gone. He finished at 1-3.

But because of his other talents, Slayback will be remembered as the most versatile man who ever played in the big leagues.

ORIGINALLY PRINTED JUNE 12, 2006.

Z-Man won't put you to sleep

I f you are a true Tigers fan, you know the players from A to Z — Glenn Abbott to George Zuverink. You also probably know that of the 1,420 players in club history through 2005, only six names begin with Z. Only Q, with George Quellich as its lonesome representative, has fewer.

The sixth Z is a 2006 rookie pitching phenom, 21-year-old, hard-throwing right-hander Joel Zumaya.

The first Tiger Z was Carl Zamloch, a right-handed pitcher. Carl, a native of Oakland, Calif., was 1-6 in 1913, his only season in the majors.

The Tigers waited 41 years before another player arrived under the Z. In 1954, Zuverink of Holland, Mich., joined the team. He had started his career with the Indians in 1951, but the Tigers obtained him from the Reds. With the Tigers in 1954-55, he was 9-18. He left for Baltimore during the 1955 season and finished his eight-year career with the Orioles. Zuverink continues to hold the distinction of being the last name in the pitcher register of the Baseball Encyclopedia.

In 1957, the only Detroit Z-man who was not a pitcher became a Tiger — slugger Gus Zernial, who broke in with the White Sox in 1949. The A's acquired him in 1951 and, after the 1957 season, traded him to the Tigers in a transaction that also

Reliever Joel Zumaya is the sixth Tiger with a last name that begins with Z. He went 6-3 with a 1.94 ERA in 2006, his rookie year.

JULIAN H. GONZALEZ

brought Billy Martin and others. Two years with the Tigers finished Zernial's career. He hit 237 home runs and had a batting average of .265.

Detroit native Bill Zepp was the Tigers' next Z pitcher. He came to Detroit in 1971 after two years with the Twins. He had a 1-1 record with the Tigers in his final season and finished his career 10-5.

Chris Zachary was the next Tiger on the Z list. A veteran right-hander, he debuted with the Astros and pitched for them in 1963-67. After stints with the A's and the Cards, he came to Detroit in 1972. In 25 games that year, he went 1-1. He finished his career the next season with Pittsburgh.

That brings us back to Zumaya. This exceptional rookie might become the best of all the Tiger Z's — a true Z-Whiz Kid.

ORIGINALLY PRINTED APRIL 24, 2006.

Zoom-Zoom better than Boom-Boom

Because he has pitched himself into the national spotlight, hard-throwing Tigers reliever Joel Zumaya deserves a nickname.

It should have an imitative sound reflecting the character of his baseball personality — his 100-m.p.h fastball that zooms past the batter.

Call him Zoom-Zoom.

Zoom-Zoom might remind fans of another Tigers pitcher, Walter (Boom-Boom) Beck, whose nickname also came from a sound of the game.

It's an old story with many versions, but the most accepted one goes this way:

On a hot, steamy afternoon in 1934, Beck was pitching for Brooklyn against the Phillies at Baker Bowl in Philadelphia. He wasn't fooling any of the batters. They kept hitting booming drives off the short rightfield wall, only 280 feet from home plate.

Recovering from a hangover, Dodgers rightfielder Hack Wilson had spent a busy afternoon chasing down these hits off the tin-covered wall. When manager Casey Stengel came to the mound to remove the inept Beck, Wilson decided he needed a quick nap. He propped himself against the wall and began his snooze.

Meanwhile, at the mound, Beck became so incensed at Stengel for taking him out of the game, he refused to give up the ball. He stepped back and heaved it toward rightfield.

When Beck's throw (maybe his best all afternoon) boomed against the wall behind Wilson, the hungover rightfielder suddenly emerged from his foggy doze. Thinking the next batter had hit still another booming drive off the wall behind him, Wilson bounced to his feet and began to chase the throw from Beck. He neatly scooped up the ball and fired an accurate throw to second base.

A bewildered Wilson looked through his blurry eyes and saw that all the Phillies and Dodgers were bent over with laughter.

Although he didn't appreciate such hilarity at that moment, Beck later accepted his nickname of Boom-Boom with grace.

When a reporter asked him if he resented everybody calling him Boom-Boom, Beck answered, "Doesn't bother me. Even my wife calls me that."

Beck was in the next-to-last season of his 12-year career in 1944 when he pitched briefly for the Tigers.

Young Zumaya is just beginning what he hopes will be a long and successful major league journey. And Zoom-Zoom has a real chance to make Tiger fans forget about Boom-Boom.

ORIGINALLY PRINTED JUNE 26, 2006.

Casey, best fidgeter in the majors

Sometimes a hitter develops his time at the plate into a production worthy of a Broadway choreographer like Bob Fosse or Gower Champion. In the process of facing the pitcher, the edgy batter fusses and fidgets enough to make coffee nervous.

My current favorite among the finest of fussy fidgeters is Tigers first baseman Sean Casey, who ranks up there with Mike (the Human Rain Delay) Hargrove and Harry (the Hat) Walker.

No batter ever outfidgeted Hargrove. His routine was the longest and most complicated. He delayed the game because he continually stepped away from the plate to go through glove-handling, shirt-tugging and bat-twirling theatrics. Whoever nick-named him the Human Rain Delay was on target.

Walker was different. He was just as nervous, but concentrated on only one extracurricular activity — cap-tugging. He wore out an average of 20 caps per season. In 1947, he also wore out National League pitchers, hitting .363 to win the batting title. Harry's brother, Dixie, had won the NL title in 1944 with a .357 average.

Sean Casey is our modern version of the mover and shaker. According to Sean, it all started because of his batting gloves.

"When I was in high school in Pennsylvania, I used to hit in the public batting cages after school," he said. "I'd do it for such a long time that my only pair of gloves got too sweaty to stay on my hands unless I stopped to tighten them. I never felt comfortable until I adjusted them. It became a habit, which I took into the games."

"What about your leg lift when you hit?" I asked.

"I started that at Kinston (N.C.) in 1996, my second year in the Cleveland system," he said. "Whenever I lifted my leg, it would pop my hip and relax me."

Casey's at-the-plate production added other frills. Eventually, he tweaked his performance for the big leagues. "I started pulling at the back of my pants and scraping dirt," he said. "Next, I added my hamstring stretch and the glove adjustment. Of course, I move the bat back and forth. All of this is to make me comfortable. Then, I'm ready for the pitch."

By the way, his first major league manager was Mike Hargrove.

ORIGINALLY PRINTED SEPT. 11, 2006.

In '40 World Series, Bobo was the story

All of us are eager to see how the 2006 World Series will rank in Tigers history. The experts have usually focused on the classics of 1909, 1934, 1935, 1968 and 1984.

Somehow, the 1940 Series between the Tigers and the Reds has been overlooked. Yet, it was one of the most interesting.

The 2006 Series intrigues me because of Bobo Newsom. Detroit was one of nine teams Bobo pitched for in his peripatetic career. He changed uniforms 16 times and served five terms with Washington. Newsom beat the Reds, 7-2, in Game 1. He won the fifth game, 8-0, the day after his dad died of a heart attack. Going for his third Series victory, Bobo turned in a strong performance in Game 7, but lost, 2-1.

A writer asked him, "Were you trying to win that one for your dad?"

"No," Newsom said. "I was trying to win it for ol' Bobo."

ORIGINALLY PRINTED OCT. 20, 2006.

'06 Tigers enjoyed magic, not Series

How will the 2006 American League champion Tigers rank in Detroit baseball history? At the moment, I'd put them below all Tigers World Series winners.

It was a magical season for the 2006 team, but its losing performance in the Series will certainly lower its rating among other Tigers teams.

However, it's almost certain that many members of the '06 pennant winners will stay for several years to give Detroit exciting baseball. They will form a nucleus for an even better team, capable of winning another pennant or two and a World Series. Such future success would enhance the '06 team's place in Tigers history

All through the season, fans have asked, "Is Jim Leyland's club as good as the 1968 and 1984 champions?"

Because the '06 team lost the World Series, the answer has to be no — not yet.

ORIGINALLY PRINTED OCT. 29, 2006.

Verlander's '06 is tough act to top

"Almost" is a word never listed in baseball records. American League rookie of the year Justin Verlander discovered that unrelenting truth in 2006.

Many rookies — especially pitchers — have found themselves cruising along the Thoroughfare of Excellence only to lose their way in Almost Alley — an alley filled with the Dumpsters and garbage cans of discarded hopes and broken dreams.

Verlander missed his chance to become the first AL rookie in more than 50 years to win 20 games. After an Aug. 1 victory, the Tigers right-hander was 14-4. With two months remaining, he seemed a cinch to be a 20-game winner. But he notched only three more victories and finished 17-9.

The last AL rookie with 20 wins was right-hander Bob Grim, who went 20-6 for the Yankees in 1954. Left-hander Tom Browning of the Reds was 20-9 in 1985, the last National League rookie to reach that goal.

Verlander almost (there's that word again) became the first Tigers rookie to win 20 in 98 years. Right-hander Ed Summers had 24 victories in 1908. The only other Detroit rookie to win 20 was right-hander Roscoe Miller, with 23 in 1901, the first year the AL was classified as a major league.

Summers' 24 victories led the Tigers in 1908. On Sept. 25 of that pennant-winning season, he pitched two complete-game victories in a doubleheader against Philadelphia. He won the opener, 7-2, then pitched 10 innings in a 1-0 nightcap.

Summers, nicknamed Kickapoo, was the first pitcher in the majors to hit two home runs in a game. His homers, in 1910, were the only two of his career.

The Tigers' staff of 1908 had not only a Summers, but a Winter. George Winter, who had pitched seven-plus years for the Red Sox before his trade in midseason to Detroit, won one game. Like Summers, Winter had a unique nickname — Sassafras.

But getting back to rookie pitchers, the most remarkable in baseball history is Grover Cleveland Alexander. In 1911, his first year with the Phillies, Alexander went 28-13. He not only led the NL in victories but also in complete games (31), innings (367) and shutouts (seven).

Don't expect Verlander to match Alexander's Hall of Fame career. But, forgetting he almost won 20, Verlander can be proud of his American League Rookie of the Year Award and pitch many fine seasons for the Tigers.

ORIGINALLY PRINTED APRIL 2, 2007.

Sam Crawford was a triple threat

C urtis Granderson's chance to set an American League record for triples in a season has projected Sam Crawford, the longtime specialist of that most elusive hit, into the spotlight.

Crawford, who shares the AL record of 26 with Shoeless Joe Jackson of the White Sox, is the career triples leader with 309.

He is the only player to lead both leagues in triples in a season. He also was the first to lead both leagues in home runs — 16 for Cincinnati in the National League in 1901 and seven for the Tigers in 1908.

Wahoo (he got his nickname from his Nebraska hometown) has another distinction. He is the only major leaguer to debut against two teams. When he started with Cincinnati in 1899, the Reds played one game that day against the Cleveland Spiders and followed with another against Louisville. Crawford got two hits in the first game, three in the second.

While with the Reds, Crawford became one of the main reasons the American League gained major league status. At a time when the American League was raiding the National League for stars, the Tigers lured Crawford away with a $3,500-a-year offer.

Reds owner Garry Herrmann was upset and reminded all parties that Crawford had already re-signed with Cincinnati. After bitter, ongoing arguments, Herrmann finally relented and Crawford became a Tiger. The owner's reconciliation was a strong move toward peace between the leagues and gave the American League equality with the National League.

In 1903, Crawford immediately established himself as a force in Detroit, hitting .335 with 25 triples, a record at that time. When Ty Cobb joined the team two years later, the duo became a powerful 1-2 batting punch but also began a lifelong feud.

Cobb claimed "Crawford never helped me in the outfield by calling 'Plenty of room' or 'You take it.' " When Cobb tried to steal second base, Crawford would foul off the pitch so Cobb would have to return to first, making the first baseman hold him closer. This ruse provided Crawford a larger hole to hit through.

The feud persisted throughout their careers. But in his mellower retirement days, Cobb successfully campaigned for Crawford's enshrinement into the Baseball Hall of Fame. Sam was inducted into Cooperstown in 1957.

The strangest twist to the Crawford story concerns his hit total. He ended his career in 1917 with 2,961 hits. Needing 39 to reach the magic mark of 3,000, Crawford retired at the age of 37. For the next four years, he played for Los Angeles in the Pacific Coast League. Over that span, he had 781 hits. But, because his hits were in the minor leagues, Crawford missed his chance at 3,000.

ORIGINALLY PRINTED AUG. 6, 2007.

Three big moves helped '72 Tigers

There is often discussion about whether the Tigers should acquire help for the stretch. To trade or not to trade? That is the question.

During the 1972 season, Tigers general manager Jim Campbell faced a similar decision. That team didn't have the glamour of Detroit's 1968 and 1984 World Series champions. But it did win the American League East with manager Billy Martin's gang of fading veterans and cast-offs.

In August of '72, Campbell made three moves that brought the title to Detroit. He added Frank Howard from Texas, Duke Sims from the Dodgers and Woodie Fryman from the Phillies.

Fryman proved to be the best addition. The 32-year-old left-hander was near the end of his trail. His Philadelphia record that season was 4-10. But he found new life with Detroit, going 10-3 and pitching a four-hitter to clinch the division.

Howard's contribution was not as spectacular, but the brawny slugger gave the Tigers some key hits and became an important factor in enhancing the winning atmosphere of Martin's clubhouse.

Sims was a journeyman catcher who sometimes played the outfield. He had never hit .300 in his career. But after batting .192 in 51 games with the Dodgers in 1972, he jumped to .316 in his 38-game, late-season stint with the Tigers.

Martin had convinced Campbell that the team had a chance to win, and the August acquisitions keyed the Tigers' stretch drive. Martin and Campbell found vindication in the success of Campbell's bold moves to strengthen his club.

The '72 Tigers put up a valiant fight but lost to Oakland in an exciting playoff series. For the next two seasons, Campbell made the mistake of depending on his fading veterans too long, and the Tigers slumped into mediocrity.

However, Detroit fans can still look back and remember fondly that time when the Tigers won in the stretch drive of '72 because of the August additions of Frank, Woodie and the Duke.

ORIGINALLY PRINTED AUG. 13, 2007.

(5)

INSIDE THE GAME

ERNIE ON BRANCH RICKEY: He was the best man at putting a dollar sign on a muscle. He could look at a guy as a prospect and figure out better than anybody else whether this guy would develop into a true major leaguer.

DISC 2, ERNIE HARWELL'S AUDIO SCRAPBOOK

Craig: 20 losses isn't the end of the world

E ven though he lost 21 games in 2003, Tigers left-hander Mike Maroth has a fine future.

That's the opinion of a qualified expert on 20-game losers. The expert is Roger Craig, who should know the subject. With the New York Mets in 1962, the first year of their existence, Roger was 10-24. He was 5-22 the next year.

"Maroth will do all right," Craig said. "He has a positive attitude and is a good learner. The Tigers asked me if, after that losing year, he should be a starter. I told them I would not hesitate to use him that way."

Craig has talked to Maroth several times. "First of all, I told him not to feel sorry for himself, but to give it his best and let the game take care of itself," Craig said.

In one of their conversations, Craig suggested to Maroth that he compare himself to Tom Glavine. "I've seen Glavine pitch a lot," Craig told him. "You have a better arm than he does, but he has a better head — because of his experience. Since you are not overpowering, you must learn the hitters and rely on your defense to keep you out of trouble."

Craig reflected on his 20-loss seasons with the Mets. "In New York, the media made a huge deal of my losing 20 games in a season," Craig said. "I remember a time when Sandy Koufax beat me, 1-0. He came into our clubhouse to congratulate me on the way I pitched. 'Yeah, and even though I beat you with a shutout,' Sandy told me, 'you have three times the number of media guys around you after the game.' That attention on losing begins to get to you. Baseball is fun most of the time, but when you keep losing, it gets to be business. You have to pitch your heart out and give your club a chance to win."

There are not many benefits in losing, but Craig found one that was very important to him.

"My losing experience helped me to understand pitchers who were not successful," he said. "I lost in so many different ways that when I became a coach and a manager, I knew exactly how those losers felt, and I could relate to them. Some guys can learn from losing. That's why I think young Maroth, who has weathered a tough season, will be all right."

ORIGINALLY PRINTED APRIL 19, 2004.

Etiquette lacking on field, but that's OK

You won't find many baseball players writing letters to Miss Manners. Yet there are unwritten rules of decorum on the diamond. Those rules are being challenged by the new-age major league player. Many have little regard for on-the-field decorum.

Away from the game, players' activities often become a report on the police docket and even in sordid headlines. That isn't our subject today. I want to explore some players' manners on the field. I think I can make the point by focusing on an event we see over and over.

Before TV gained a stranglehold on baseball, a batter hit a home run, circled the bases and touched home plate. It was as simple as that. Then came Reggie Jackson. When Reggie drilled one, he would stand in the batter's box for a dramatic moment and admire his handiwork.

Now many hitters embroider their homers with the same Jacksonian flair. In earlier days, such behavior would have invited a knockdown pitch during the show-off's next plate appearance. Not anymore.

Tigers Hall of Famer Al Kaline has an explanation.

"When I played," he says, "we never wanted to

embarrass the opposition. I knew if I showed up the pitcher with a big home run trot, he would knock me down the next time he pitched to me. Now the players don't retaliate. So they can give it the long look of admiration when they hit a homer."

Tigers coach Juan Samuel says during his rookie year, veteran players schooled younger players on baseball etiquette. "With the Phillies, Joe Morgan, Pete Rose, Mike Schmidt, Garry Maddox and Gary Matthews all helped me. I've always tried to teach the Latinos how to act," Samuel said.

"They are facing new experiences in a new culture, and they need to be instructed. It's not an easy transition for them. I tell these youngsters not to embarrass players on the other team. If they do that, it will come back to haunt them."

Yes, baseball does have its own etiquette. My opinion is this: I don't want to take color from the game. I like to see enthusiasm and aggressiveness. We don't need a game of vanilla. I don't feel that to challenge the opposition by showing off is all that bad.

What do you think? Or maybe we should write Miss Manners.

ORIGINALLY PRINTED APRIL 26, 2004.

All-Star Game is still alluring

I remember baseball's first All-Star Game. On that afternoon, July 6, 1933, I was an excited 15-year-old, hanging on every word of the radio broadcast from Comiskey Park in Chicago. Since then, I've listened to or watched most of the other All-Star matchups. I've even broadcast four of them. It is still the best All-Star attraction of any sport, mainly because the rules are not changed for this one game and there is still true competition between the leagues. In other sports, teams representing two divisions of the same league play each other.

The '33 game was not actually the first. All-Stars competed against each other as far back as 1858. Stars from various Brooklyn teams played stars of New York teams in a three-game series at Fashion Race Course, near Jamaica, N.Y. Despite rumors to the contrary, I didn't see those games, hear them on the radio or broadcast them.

What I remember best about that first game in '33 was Babe Ruth's home run. It beat the team I was rooting for, the National Leaguers, 4-2. Years later, veteran Tigers super-scout Rick Ferrell talked about catching the entire game, certainly an unusual feat in All-Star history.

In 1932, Ferrell hit a career-high .315 for the St.

Louis Browns. But in May 1933, the Browns sent him to the Boston Red Sox. It was Boston's first deal under the Tom Yawkey regime.

"I was really surprised when manager Connie Mack told me I was catching for the American League All-Stars," Rick told me. "Lefty Gomez was our starting pitcher, so I thought surely Mr. Mack would use Lefty's Yankee batterymate, Bill Dickey."

Compared with the current game, there was almost no ballyhoo. The players arrived by train the night before and left as soon as the game ended. Ferrell couldn't remember if the players received gifts for their appearances.

"I think we each got a ring, worth about $25," he said.

Many of the owners didn't like the idea of an All-Star Game. But their opposition could not withstand pressure from Arch Ward, sports editor of the powerful Chicago Tribune and the originator of the idea.

The event proved a great success and has become a true sports fixture.

ORIGINALLY PRINTED JULY 12, 2004.

Samuel still gets flak for ill-timed bunt

I always enjoy talking with Tigers third-base coach Juan Samuel. He has keen baseball insight — from the standpoint of player and coach. He has a shining personality and hundreds of friends in the game. He is especially valuable to the Tigers because he relates so well to Latin players.

Sammy and I were discussing some of the no-nos of the game. For instance, a batter doesn't swing at a 3-0 pitch when his team has a huge lead. Or it's not right to steal a base when your team is way ahead.

"What about bunting when the opposing pitcher is going for a no-hitter?" I asked him. Sammy smiled.

"Funny you got around to that one," he said. "Because I did that once. In fact, it was not only a no-hitter, it was a perfect game."

He explained: "When I was with the Los Angeles Dodgers in 1991, Dennis Martinez — that terrific pitcher from Nicaragua — was on the mound for Montreal. We were behind, 2-0. I was not aware that Dennis had a perfect game going. ... A game like that goes very fast, so when I came up to bat, I just didn't know. I was concentrating on trying to get on base. We couldn't touch the guy. He was pitching great. I had to try something. So I laid down a bunt toward third. It was a good bunt, but Dennis charged off the mound, grabbed the ball and fired to first base — just in time to get me.

"I still think it was a good move. I wasn't trying to show up Dennis. I didn't even know about the perfect game. I was so absorbed in my time at bat — trying to get on base and get something started against him — that the perfect game wasn't even in my mind. Well, he went on to get his perfect game. Some people didn't like my bunting in that situation. They told me it was against an unwritten rule of the game. I took some flak about it, but I still believe it was OK to do — even if I had known about Dennis' perfect game.

"That happened 13 years ago, but now whenever I'm in Miami, some of Martinez's Nicaraguan friends still kid me about that bunt. They just don't forget."

ORIGINALLY PRINTED AUG. 30, 2004.

Rain delays can produce zany at-bats

T he worst thing that can happen in a baseball game is a rain delay. It takes the starch out of everybody — manager, coaches, players, fans and media. Only the concessionaires welcome the delay. It gives them a chance to sell more beer, pop, hot dogs and popcorn.

A rain delay led to one of the goofiest at-bats I ever broadcast.

It involved one of my all-time favorites, Clint Courtney, the feisty catcher of the Baltimore Orioles. He became a strikeout victim in the most prolonged strikeout ever recorded.

On a wet and dreary afternoon, the Orioles were playing the Chicago White Sox at Memorial Stadium in Baltimore. A light rain had been falling throughout the game. It was still raining when Courtney batted in the last of the ninth against Harry Dorish. With the Sox leading, 4-3, the O's had Jim Brideweser on second base and Jim Fridley on first base with two outs.

Baltimore's hopes were high. Courtney was the team's best clutch hitter. He had struck out only twice during the first two-thirds of the season. Now the rain was getting worse. When the count reached 3-2, Courtney stepped away from the plate. Rain increased in intensity until it became a storm.

Plate umpire Jim Honochick looked at the sky and gave up. He waved the players off the field and signaled for the grounds crew to get to work. Only one more pitch, one more strike, and the game would end. But the rain was so heavy that Honochick had no choice but to stop play.

Thus began the rain delay. It lasted 1:07.

Finally, the rain stopped, the field was prepared, and play resumed. Courtney took his stance at the plate. Dorish threw a fastball over the plate, just above the knees. Courtney froze and took the pitch for strike three. The game was over. Clint had failed, fanning for the third time that season.

After the game, Courtney was undaunted.

"Yeah," he said. "Dorish struck me out, but it took him over an hour to get me."

ORIGINALLY PRINTED SEPT. 6, 2004.

Tigers lack that rival team to hate

Tigers fans need a team to hate. They need the passion of a Yankees-Red Sox or Giants-Dodgers rivalry.

Other cities have rivalries like these, but not Detroit.

Feuding franchises build attendance, evidenced by the first weekend of interleague play. Without a rival, the Tigers find their interleague schedule no more attractive to fans than a normal regular-season game. While the Tigers were hosting the Arizona Diamondbacks, other cities were reaping attendance benefits from their rivalries. Check out these series: Mets-Yankees, Cubs-White Sox, Athletics-Giants, Angels-Dodgers, Astros-Rangers, Reds-Indians and Cardinals-Royals. These matchups are created by geography and a fight for regional bragging rights.

A Tigers-Diamondbacks series lacks what local fans need in interleague play. Arizona beat the Yankees in a thrilling 2001 World Series. But based several time zones away, the Diamondbacks don't qualify as rivals. Neither do the other National League teams scheduled to play the Tigers in 2005. In June, the Tigers visit the Dodgers in Los Angeles, the Rockies in Denver and the Diamondbacks in Phoenix. National League teams appearing at Comerica Park will be the San Diego Padres and the San Francisco Giants. Like Arizona, these distant teams have no Detroit connection.

The depth of the missing rivalry problem that besets the Tigers is more severe in American League play. Tigers fans can only dream of a Yankees-Red Sox type of feud. Detroit needs another baseball city on which fans can unleash their impassioned hatred.

The Tigers had a touch of this kind of rivalry that grew from their battle with the Indians for the pennant in 1940. Pitching duels between Hall of Famers Bob Feller of Cleveland and Hal Newhouser highlighted that competition.

In the mid-1980s, when the Tigers and Toronto Blue Jays had some meaningful battles, a near rivalry began to emerge but soon died when the Tigers fell on hard times while the Blue Jays won back-to-back World Series in 1992-93.

ORIGINALLY PRINTED MAY 23, 2005.

Today's players are as good as ever

f people ask me to compare modern players with old-timers, they usually expect me to go on about the good old days. I tell them the good old days are now. Baseball is as good as ever.

Sure, there have been changes — good and bad. But today's players are equal to those I saw in the late 1940s — an era many consider baseball's golden age.

But the current players' reputations suffer because everybody likes to glorify the past. We remember the good times in school with our pals and forget the drudgery of the classroom. In music, we cherish the old songs yet overlook the bad tunes. And in baseball we glorify the stars of yesterday but dismiss the mediocre players of the time.

Here are quotes to enlighten the then vs. now:

■ "Salaries must come down or the interest of the public must be increased in some way. If one or other does not happen, bankruptcy stares every team in the face." — Albert Spalding, 1881.

■ "No clan of men on the face of the globe earn their money easier than the professional baseball players, as they only work two hours a day when they work at all, and their salaries vary from 50 to 150 dollars a week. Still they are constantly complaining of being overworked and they have to be coaxed and humored like a lot of spoiled children. Why, were it not for baseball, the majority of these whiners and complainers would not be able to make a living, as they are too infernally lazy to make a success even at carrying a hod. If the managers only had the backbone to lay every one of these lazy whelps off without pay and fill their places with younger blood, or crowd them out of the business altogether, it will work a radical change and give the public baseball exhibitions well worth seeing." — The National Police Gazette, Oct. 16, 1886.

■ "The players of today are not like those of my day. In my day, such a little thing as a charley horse, a sprain or bad hand would not keep a man out of the game. Now, they get out for the least thing and stay out when, for all appearances, they are able to play ball."— Jimmy Manning, 1901.

■ "Baseball has been deteriorating for the past 10 years." — Charlie Comiskey, 1902.

■ "Baseball today is not what it used to be. The players do not try to learn all the fine points of the game but simply try to get by. They content themselves if they get a couple of hits or play an errorless game. It makes me weep to think of the men of the old days — and the boys of today. It's positively a shame that they are getting money for it, too." — Bill Joyce, 1916.

Throughout baseball history, the older generation has maintained that its era was the best.

ORIGINALLY PRINTED JULY 25, 2005.

Sharp eyes on the diamond

"You're blind, ump" was a lyric from a song from the musical "Damn Yankees." Although that sardonic accusation has echoed throughout baseball history, seldom has any complainant taken strong action.

One notable exception came during the 1999 American League Championship Series between the Yankees and Red Sox. Umpiring decisions against Boston prompted world-renowned ophthalmologist Carmen Puliafito to put his money where his mouth was, offering free eye exams, prescription lenses and laser surgery to the culprits.

"The umpires have created a crisis, and emergency actions are needed," said Puliafito, then director of New England Eye Center at Tufts University School of Medicine. "I'm willing to give away these services to ensure the Sox a fair shot at the World Series."

Although no umpires accepted Puliafito's offer, national press, TV and radio featured it. Paul Harvey highlighted the item, and the story made headlines everywhere.

Dr. Puliafito has since become chairman of Bascom Palmer Eye Institute in Miami, one of the most prestigious in the nation. Lecturing all over the world, he has built a worthy reputation. Yet

JULIAN H. GONZALEZ

Tigers Gary Sheffield, left, and Placido Polanco might disagree on this play, but umps, such as Derryl Cousins here, are not blind.

none of his work has ever attracted the same attention as his offer to the umpires.

Despite what frustrated eye doctors, fans, players and managers might think, umpires aren't blind. Unless you cite my sightless friend Elmer Kapp of Plymouth, who has been umpire-in-chief at Tigers fantasy camps.

Almost all discussions of blindness are tinged with good humor — even among the umps themselves. When Lee Weyer took a medical examination, the doctor told him he was suffering from Guillain-Barre syndrome, which sometimes leads to blindness.

"This means you will not be able to umpire anymore," the doctor said.

"Why not?" Weyer asked. "Being blind has never

stopped me before."

Weyer kept working until he retired in 1988 after a 27-year career in the National League.

Other umpires are more sensitive than Weyer. When I began my big-league broadcasting career in 1948, several of the veterans were in their 50s or older and probably had bad vision. They always refused to have eye examinations. Although they might have worn glasses in private, they would not dare wear them at work.

Later, umpires began to disregard such a stigma. Eddie Rommel became the first to wear glasses in a game, on April 18, 1956. Eddie had worn glasses for years but never during a game. After Rommel broke the barrier, Frank Umont, Larry Goetz and Al Clark umpired wearing corrective lenses.

No present-day major league umpires wear glasses at work. The number wearing contacts is a trade secret.

I've always admired umpires. They protect baseball at its most crucial point, the diamond.

The modern group is superior to umpires of the past. They're in better shape, more dedicated and less confrontational.

Placing umpires under the commissioner's office was an excellent move. And TV replays have proved their decisions correct more often than we ever anticipated.

Let's not be blind to the great contribution umpires make to baseball.

ORIGINALLY PRINTED MAY 15, 2006.

Pitch count notion isn't anything new

Whom can we blame for inflicting us with the pitch count? I am blaming Paul Richards. The first time I encountered the pitch count was in 1958, when Orioles manager Richards imposed the restriction on his rookie right-hander from Detroit Cooley High, 19-year-old Milt Pappas.

I called the 67-year-old Pappas at his Beecher, Ill., home to ask him about the circumstances surrounding Richards' innovation.

"When did you find out that Paul was going to restrict your number of pitches?" I asked.

"Right in the middle of a game," Pappas said. "Richards had never mentioned pitch count to me until he came out to the mound."

On May 4, 1958, his first full season with Baltimore, Pappas suffered an injured arm pitching against the Tigers. So the Orioles put him on the 15-day disabled list.

In a start after his reactivation, he was pitching a shutout. Then, after 80 pitches, Richards came to the mound.

"I came here to get you," he told Pappas.

"Whattaya mean?" Pappas asked.

"You've thrown 80 pitches. That's enough," Richards said. "I don't want you hurting that arm again. You're gone."

Pappas pitched another month under the restriction. When the rookie's arm was OK again, Richards canceled the pitch count.

"My arm was fine after that," Pappas said. "Never had any arm trouble the rest of my career."

His career started with a highly publicized signing bonus on June 26, 1957, at the age of 18. Pappas made his debut Aug. 10 of that year at Yankee Stadium, and he blanked the New Yorkers in two innings of relief.

"The first four batters I faced," he said, "were Enos Slaughter, Mickey Mantle, Yogi Berra and Moose Skowron."

Pappas pitched four games for Baltimore that first season — a total of nine innings. In 1958, still a rookie, he finished with a 10-10 record. His career lasted 17 seasons. He won 209 games for Baltimore, Cincinnati, Atlanta and the Chicago Cubs. He retired at 34.

When Richards limited Pappas to 80 pitches per game in 1958, it was the first time I had encountered the pitch count. That was almost 50 years ago. Now, the craze has permeated baseball. Managers and pitching coaches can't leave home without it.

ORIGINALLY PRINTED APRIL 9, 2007.

Eck said it, and the walk-off was born

"How did the expression walk-off home run get started?" That was the question from my 92-year-old friend, Ward Stoddard. Ward is a musician, world traveler, raconteur, entrepreneur and business consultant. But, most of all, he is the consummate baseball fan. His avidity toward the game is symbolized by his record of attending 61 straight Tiger openers.

Ward's question about the walk-off homer reflects the curiosity of many baseball followers.

So, I began to dig for an answer, discovering that the talented Dan Shaughnessy of the Boston Globe had written about the subject in June 2005. First, let's get a definition from the New Dickson Baseball Dictionary: "... A walk-off piece is a home run that wins the game and the pitcher walks off the mound." The dictionary traces first use of the term to July 30, 1988, by Gannett News Service. The phrase was the invention of Hall of Fame pitcher Dennis Eckersley. The first walk-off reference appeared several months before Kirk Gibson hit one of the most famous walk-off homers — off Eckersley himself.

Gibby's blast put the spotlight on Eckersley and the walk-off. ESPN took it from there, making it a common phrase in baseball's lexicon. "I hate to take the credit," Eck told Shaughnessy. "It's not a good thing for a pitcher. You don't want to be known for giving it up. I'd hate to be the one talking about walk-offs like I was the master of them."

But Eckersley is established as the inventor of the phrase. It was just one example of his mastery of the colorful expression, a technique he claims he learned from former Tigers pitcher Pat Dobson.

Anyway, the walk-off home run is with us — for better or for worse. In my opinion, it's for worse, because of its negative connotation. A home run should be celebrated from the standpoint of the hitter. Instead, the expression walk-off puts the onus on the pitcher. Besides, walk-off is a weak word to describe such an exciting, he-man accomplishment as a home run — especially a game-winner.

How do you feel about it? Let me know.

ORIGINALLY PRINTED MAY 7, 2007.

Stealing home is a lost art

Whatever happened to stealing home? Once baseball's most exciting play, it is almost forgotten. It's a play I never forget — because in 1948 during the first inning of my first major league broadcast, Jackie Robinson stole home.

Several elements contribute to the excitement of the steal of home. It usually happens in a close game. The key to its success is surprise, and depends on daring, speed and elusiveness.

Aaron Hill of the Blue Jays gave the Toronto crowd a rare thrill May 29, 2007, when he stole home against Yankees left-hander Andy Pettitte.

With the score 1-1 in the seventh, Hill was on third base with Jason Phillips on first. Hill stole home, but Phillips stayed at first, making it a pure steal of home, not the front end of a double-steal. A double-steal is exciting, but it lacks the rarity and thrill of a straight steal of home.

The pure type has disappeared because of an emphasis on the home run and the big inning. Most managers would rather depend on a big slugger and wait for the three-run homer.

Hall of Famer Rod Carew is the most recent expert at stealing home. Although a seven-time batting champion, he also was a talented baserunner.

FREE PRESS FILE PHOTO

Tiger Ty Cobb owns the record for stealing home the most times in a season (eight) and a career (50). It's a rarity today, though.

Carew stole home seven times in 1969 — the same number Dodgers outfielder Pete Reiser posted in 1946.

The all-time record of eight in a season belongs to Ty Cobb of the Tigers in 1912. Cobb also holds the major league record for lifetime steals of home with 50. Max Carey owns the National League mark with 33.

These speedsters dominated an era of inside baseball, when home runs were rare and runs were scratched out by speed and trickery.

When Robinson arrived on the scene with the Dodgers in 1947, he was a throwback to that era. He created a newfound excitement with his baserunning.

Robinson was the most exciting player I ever saw. Dancing off a base, he would draw a throw that would skip past the fielder, allowing him to take the next base. He often would get caught in a rundown, but somehow managed to escape because some infielder would toss away the ball. Robinson always was a threat. He was constantly upsetting the pitcher and defense with his daring on the bases.

You've probably seen him as the central figure in one of baseball's most famous photos. The scene is Robinson stealing home in the 1955 World Series against the Yankees. Catcher Yogi Berra is there, too, ready to protest the call.

It's a true picture of baseball's most exciting play — the straight steal of home. Too bad we don't have a chance to enjoy the rare event anymore.

ORIGINALLY PRINTED JULY 16, 2007.

(6)

ALL ABOUT THE PLAYERS

ERNIE ON JACKIE ROBINSON: He was probably a lot better football, basketball, track star than he was a baseball player, but he applied himself so much. He had terrific drive, terrific ambition, and he was the most exciting player that I think I ever saw. **"**

DISC 2, ERNIE HARWELL'S AUDIO SCRAPBOOK

Bonds, Babe in league of their own

Sometimes, as a reader, you get zapped by a most inconsequential statement. Once, I was reading a great article comparing the records of Barry Bonds and Babe Ruth.

The sentence was lost in a long paragraph near the end of the story. It was even in parentheses.

"(Ruth was not walked intentionally once in his entire career)." That's what it said.

Wait a minute, I told myself, that can't be right. Such a statement seems impossible. The home run king of his era was a feared hitter. Surely, he was intentionally walked many times.

Didn't I read somewhere long ago that the Babe's nemesis, Hub Pruett, once walked him intentionally with the bases loaded?

So I phoned my old pal Seymour Siwoff, president of the Elias Sports Bureau, official record keeper for the major leagues.

What about it? I asked him. Was the Babe ever walked intentionally?

"Of course he was," Seymour said. "The problem is this. Here is one category where nobody can compare Ruth and Bonds because no stats were officially kept on intentional walks until the season of 1955 — 20 years after Babe's retirement. Thus, no one can ever prove how many intentional walks

Ruth received."

Until Bonds, the record for intentional walks in a season belonged to San Francisco's Willie McCovey — 45 in 1969. Bonds shattered that mark with 68 in 2002.

(Bonds broke his own record with 120 intentional walks in 2004, and by the end of the 2007 season, he had 688 career intentional walks.)

All of these figures highlight the fact that Bonds dominates a game more than any other hitter in history. In the early 1900s, Ty Cobb filled that role. In the '20s and '30s, it was Ruth. Now, it is Bonds.

He seldom gets a pitch to hit, and the entire game becomes an exercise in how to keep the guy from beating you almost single-handedly.

Maybe the ultimate tribute to Bonds' hitting prowess came May 28, 1998, when he was intentionally walked with the bases loaded by Arizona's Gregg Olson. The next batter, Brent Mayne, lined out to end the game, an 8-7 loss for the Giants.

ORIGINALLY PRINTED MAY 10, 2004.

Sisler's start came at U-M with Rickey

I t was a strange sight. Duke Snider, the young Brooklyn Dodgers outfielder, was in the batting cage without a bat. Behind the cage stood an elderly gentleman, assessing Snider's judgment of the strike zone.

After each pitch, George Sisler would ask young Snider, "Ball or strike?" In the early going, Duke's answer disagreed with Sisler's idea of the strike zone. As the workout continued, the youngster began to learn the difference between ball and strike from his legendary coach.

That scene at Vero Beach, Fla., spring training in 1949 was my introduction to Sisler. Although I had known of his playing exploits, I'd never met him. What a kind and intelligent man he was.

In 2004, Seattle's Ichiro Suzuki amassed 262 hits, breaking Sisler's record, set in 1920, of 257 in a season. As Suzuki's quest unfolded, modern fans began wondering: "Who was George Sisler?"

Let me tell you, he was a true Hall of Famer with an amazing career. Yet, of all baseball superstars, this modest man is the least celebrated.

Ty Cobb called Sisler "the nearest thing to a perfect ballplayer." Sisler's college coach and dear friend, Branch Rickey, said: "He is the smartest hitter that ever lived. He was a picture player, the acme of grace and fluency."

George's lifetime batting average was .340. He won two batting titles, hitting above .400 each time. For 13 seasons he batted better than .300, and in 1922, had a 41-game hitting streak. He struck out only 14 times that season in 586 times at bat. Sisler led the American League in stolen bases four times and was considered the game's top fielding first baseman. Graceful but not flashy, he had a modest demeanor that attracted few headlines.

Sisler was a pitcher when he reported for a try-out with the University of Michigan team. The coach was Rickey, who couldn't believe how this freshman dominated the older players. He once fanned 20 in an intrasquad game. From the Michigan campus, George went straight to the big leagues. He broke in with the St. Louis Browns in 1915, alternating as pitcher, first baseman and out-fielder.

Sisler's magnificent career would have been even greater except for illness. In 1923 a case of flu attacked his sinuses, leaving him with double vision, a condition so severe that he had to sit out the entire 1923 season. He never completely recovered.

In 1924, Sisler became the Browns' playing manager but lasted only two years with a bad team. He was sold to Washington for the 1927 season and finished with the Boston Braves in 1929-30.

George returned to baseball in the mid-'40s to scout for Rickey, president and general manager of the Dodgers. When Rickey moved to Pittsburgh, George accompanied him and was a Pirates scout and batting instructor.

Although Sisler never made big headlines during his career, he got back in the news because of Ichiro's chase.

ORIGINALLY PRINTED SEPT. 13, 2004.

Classy Olerud should boost Boston

'm a longtime admirer of John Olerud, so I welcome his return to the major leagues — this time with the Boston Red Sox.

Over the years you get to know and appreciate certain players, and Olerud is a good example.

He is one of the classiest athletes I've known. He is also a true pro — a graceful, talented first baseman and a hitter with a picture-perfect swing. Olerud could never run with the base-stealing rabbits, and I'm sure that reaching the age of 36 has not increased his speed. But he will be a true asset to manager Terry Francona — a quiet, calming influence in a frenetic clubhouse.

Olerud was with the New York Yankees in 2004, but he suffered an injured foot in the playoffs against Boston. The Yankees released him, and he signed with the Red Sox.

Because his foot didn't heal until a month after spring training, his first action came late in May with the Gulf Coast Red Sox. He went 8-for-10, then moved to Triple-A Pawtucket for a couple of games. It was the first time Olerud had played in the minor leagues.

He had gone straight from Washington State to the major leagues with the Toronto Blue Jays. His dad, a dermatologist and onetime minor league catcher, had groomed his son for stardom. Young Olerud was a college phenom but suffered a brain aneurysm while at Washington State.

After brain surgery, his athletic future was dim. He still wanted to play pro baseball, but most clubs didn't want to risk the danger. Dr. Olerud gave his son permission to play, if he would take the precaution of wearing a helmet on the bases.

Olerud rewarded the Blue Jays for their confidence in signing him. His steady bat and top-notch fielding helped Toronto win the World Series in 1992 and 1993. It was with the Blue Jays that Olerud enjoyed his best year — 1993, when he flirted with .400 in August and won the American League batting title with a .363 average.

After Toronto, his career took Olerud to the New York Mets, Seattle and the Yankees before joining the Red Sox.

I think he'll be good for Boston, but I will always link Olerud with the team that took a chance on him — the Blue Jays.

ORIGINALLY PRINTED JUNE 6, 2005.

Robinsons rule in Hall of Fame

The best name in the history of baseball is Robinson. You could start with Jackie. His breaking of the color line in the mid-'40s is the most significant event not only in baseball but in the history of all sports.

The Hall of Fame roster attests to the greatness of the other Robinsons — Wilbert, Frank and Brooks. Of those four, only Wilbert was not elected in his first year of eligibility.

And to emphasize the Robby dominance, no other name of a player is represented more in those hallowed halls of Cooperstown, N.Y.

There are three Williamses — Ted, Billy and Negro Leaguer Joe. Names of players listed twice in the Hall of Fame include Reggie and Travis Jackson, Paul and Lloyd Waner, Eddie and Jimmy Collins, George and King Kelly, and George and Harry Wright.

None compare with the Robinsons. Let's look at this clan in thumbnail fashion.

WILBERT ROBINSON

Catcher for the Baltimore Orioles of the 1890s, a team famous for innovative strategy and competitive toughness. Set a record in 1892 with seven hits in a nine-inning game. Longtime Brooklyn manager, leading his team to its first two World Series, in 1916 and 1920.

JACKIE ROBINSON

This Dodgers trailblazer led his team to six National League pennants in his 10 seasons. Was the NL's MVP in his best year, 1949. Led the league in hitting that season with a .342 mark and drove in 124 runs. Featured an exciting baserunning style and stole home 19 times in his career.

FRANK ROBINSON

He is the only player named MVP in each major league (with the Reds in 1961 and the Orioles in 1966). An aggressive-hitting outfielder and talented baserunner. Hit 586 home runs. Frank was the first African American to manage in the big leagues, breaking that barrier with Cleveland in 1975. He also has managed the San Francisco Giants, Baltimore Orioles, Montreal Expos and Washington Nationals.

BROOKS ROBINSON

Won the American League MVP in 1964 with his steady hitting and outstanding work at third base. Was World Series MVP in 1970, batting .429 and sparkling with his glove. In 23 years with the Orioles, the "Human Vacuum Cleaner" took fielding prowess to a new level. He revived that old gag about the third baseman, customizing it this way: "The batter hit a double down the leftfield line, and Robinson threw him out at first base."

ORIGINALLY PRINTED AUG. 1, 2005.

Detroit slugger wronged by records

B aseball record keepers have twice wronged Sam Thompson, the Detroit Wolverines' super slugger who played in the 1880s and '90s.

First, in 1921, Sam was officially recognized as the leader in career home runs when Babe Ruth surpassed him. That recognition was switched from Sam to Roger Connor because researchers restored 14 home runs from the Players League to Connor's total.

Second, the Hall of Fame and all record books list Thompson as a left-handed-throwing outfielder, but the Thompson family claims it has proof he threw right-handed.

Of all Detroit Hall of Famers who were elected as players, Thompson reaches deepest into the past. His lifetime average is .331, and he batted .407 in 1894. He collected 200 or more hits in three seasons and twice led the National League in homers and RBIs.

In RBIs per game, Thompson is the all-time best. He knocked in almost one run per game for his career. His mark was .921 — better than Lou Gehrig (.920), Hank Greenberg (.915), Joe DiMaggio (.885) and Ruth (.821).

Of the two controversies concerning Thompson,

it is easier to understand the home run issue. The Players League, which lasted one year (1890), was long considered a minor league. When the experts gave it major league status, Thompson lost his home run crown.

The stranger quirk is this: Despite his fame and baseball's proclivity for minutiae, nobody knows with which arm Thompson threw. The family insists he threw right-handed.

Thompson was honored in 2006 with a historical marker at his hometown of Danville, Ind., in a ceremony marking the 100th anniversary of Thompson's final major league game when the Tigers pressed him into a comeback at the age of 46. The Thompson family was represented by Sam's great nephews: Don, Chuck and Keith Thompson.

Don Thompson told me: "My dad, Lawrence Thompson, hunted and fished with Sam, and always said Sam hunted and fished right-handed."

The most telling evidence came from researcher Steve DeHoff, who found this item in the Philadelphia Inquirer: "Sam Thompson proved not only that he is a good fielder, but that he has not lost use of his right arm. He threw out a runner at the plate and made two splendid line throws from extreme rightfield to third base."

When I was in Cooperstown, I found that same item in the Hall of Fame archives. Strangely enough, most references to Thompson's great throwing ability do not say which arm he used.

Also, I discovered that in its extensive files, the Hall has no photos of Thompson with a glove.

So, although there are family pleas and evidence to the contrary, Thompson remains officially a left-handed thrower.

Despite this unresolved question and Thompson's loss of his home run crown, the Detroit slugger was truly a superstar of baseball history.

ORIGINALLY PRINTED JUNE 19, 2006.

Sultan's final swats are lasting memory

How's this for coincidence? I'm writing a column that goes like this: "I'm looking for some Babe stories. I don't mean a Babe dancer or a Babe in the bar. I mean stories about the Baseball Babe, George Herman Ruth."

My wife, Lulu, walks into the room with mail forwarded from Comerica Park. In the packet is a letter from Donald Oatman Sr. of Holly. Don wrote that he was at Forbes Field in Pittsburgh for a significant moment in the life of Babe Ruth.

"As a 13-year-old usher on May 25, 1935," he wrote, "I saw Babe, then with the Boston Braves, hit the final three home runs of his career."

At a concession stand before the game, Oatman watched Ruth eat four hot dogs and wash them down with soda pop. Then he got Babe's autograph on a piece of paper.

Oatman began to usher, pausing to watch the game. Ruth homered off Red Lucas in his first at-bat. Babe hit another home run off Guy Bush. Then he singled.

In the seventh, Bush fired a fastball and Babe lifted a tremendous drive over the rightfield roof. It was home run No. 714 and the final in Babe's career. The drive was the longest in Forbes Field history and the first to clear the 86-foot-high roof.

FREE PRESS FILE PHOTO

Babe Ruth, left, shown here with Ty Cobb, hit his final three homers in a game at Pittsburgh's Forbes Field in 1935.

Oatman practically grew up at Forbes Field.

"My first job was retrieving baseballs," he said. "My brother Robert and I chased balls and talked fans into returning them to the team. In those days, clubs didn't allow anybody to keep a ball."

After his dramatic homer outburst, those closest to Ruth, then 40, urged him to retire. But he resisted pleas from his wife, Claire; his agent, Christy Walsh and his former teammate Duffy Lewis, the Braves' traveling secretary.

Five days later, he had not collected another hit. Hurt and tired, Ruth walked off the field in the first inning of a doubleheader at Philadelphia. He would never play again.

His three-homer explosion in Pittsburgh had been his final big bang.

Meanwhile, young Oatman graduated from Schenley High School. He ushered at Duquesne Gardens and later served as its night watchman. In World War II, Don became an 8th Army Air Force B-17 pilot. He and his crew were shot down over occupied France, but he escaped to fly 35 missions.

During the war, Don married Helen Elizabeth Smith and later moved to Detroit.

The 13-year-old usher who had watched Ruth's last home run hurrah in Pittsburgh was a grown man when he next saw the frail home run king.

"Babe was at a golf tournament in Detroit with Sammy Byrd," Oatman said. "He sat in a Lincoln Continental convertible swigging beer. It was sad to realize this American hero was near death. Looking back, I accept the reality that Babe is not the home run king anymore and that I've lost his autograph. But I still cherish the memory of watching his final three home runs."

ORIGINALLY PRINTED JULY 17, 2006.

Mauer has batting title shot as catcher

t has never happened in the 106-year history of the American League, but Minnesota's Joe Mauer is going for it.

He might become the first AL catcher to win a batting championship. He also has a good chance of surpassing the highest average of any major league catcher — Bill Dickey's .362 for the Yankees in 1936.

When you think about all the great American League catchers, it's difficult to realize that none was a batting champion. Dickey and Mickey Cochrane came close. In 1936, Luke Appling of the White Sox hit .388, topping Dickey's .362. In 1930, Cochrane was beaten by Athletics teammate Al Simmons, .381 to .357.

Two National League catchers have won batting titles, Bubbles Hargrave and Ernie Lombardi. Hargrave hit .353 with Cincinnati in 1926. Lombardi won the title twice, hitting .342 for the Reds in 1938 and .330 for the Boston Braves in 1942.

Joe Torre won the NL batting championship with the Cardinals — but not as a catcher. After catching for the first 11 years of his career, Torre switched to third base. In his first full season at the hot corner (1971), he batted .363 to win the title.

Of the 15 catchers in the Hall of Fame, four have lifetime averages higher than .300: Cochrane, 320;

JULIAN H. GONZALEZ

The Twins' Joe Mauer, shown here with Tiger Sean Casey, became the first AL catcher to win a batting title in 2006. He hit .347.

Dickey, .313; Lombardi, .306 and Buck Ewing, .303.

When Tigers catcher Ivan Rodriguez makes the Hall of Fame, he might join this select .300 group. Pudge began the 2006 season with a lifetime average of .304. Another current possibility is Mike Piazza, who started 2006 at .311. If Piazza becomes a Hall of Famer, he will be the Hall's first catcher with more than 400 home runs. The current leader is Johnny Bench with 389.

Of all the catchers who have a lifetime average of .300, only one is not in the Hall of Fame: Virgil (Spud) Davis, who batted .308 in his 16-year National League career.

Editor's note: Mauer went on to win the batting title in 2006 with an average of .347.

ORIGINALLY PRINTED AUG. 7, 2006.

Mourning a true gentleman

Elden Auker was a man's man. Yet when his son phoned me with news of his father's death, one word came to mind — "gentle."

It seems incongruous to describe the old underhanded pitcher who competed in that rough-tough Depression era of baseball as gentle. But, above all, Elden was gentle.

To show you how gentle he was, I'll get personal with a confession.

Earlier in the 2006 season, I wrote a column about Elden, one of my heroes — 95 years old, still brimming with love of life. He possessed an innate curiosity, a man of many interests. He had pitched in the big leagues and made many friends. He loved to play golf with Babe Ruth and bridge with Dizzy Dean. He was a successful businessman.

I always enjoyed my phone conversations with Elden, and it was a joy to get his handwritten letters. Yes, he was a real hero.

So I wrote a column about him in May 2006. Because of the mistakes I made, the column became an embarrassment. Elden and I always had laughed about how often his first name was misspelled. That was the theme of my column.

I knew his name was correctly spelled Elden and not the often-used Eldon.

So what did I do? I wrote Eldon throughout the piece. Also, I noted that Auker (not Eddie Mayo) was the oldest surviving Tiger. At that point, I was 0-for-2.

After the column ran in the Free Press, I got a phone call from Elden. "Ernie," he said, "thank you for writing such a nice column about me. People from all over the country have been calling. I really appreciate it."

I was flattered by his call. "Thanks," I said, "but I want to apologize to you for misspelling your name."

"Oh, that's all right," he said. "You know, a lot of people are always spelling my name incorrectly. And, Ernie, I want you to know that I didn't even mind that you got my wife Mildred's name wrong when you called her Margaret."

This man Elden Auker was gentle — truly gentle.

ORIGINALLY PRINTED AUG. 14, 2006.

Tigers hurler writes with perspective

Todd (Roller Coaster) Jones is a favorite of mine. He is frank, open and sincere. Win or lose, he doesn't dodge media scrutiny. He is like Sal (The Barber) Maglie, my close friend who pitched for the New York Giants in the 1950s. If Maglie pitched a bad game, he'd admit it. If he was good, he would tell you why. Few major league pitchers are like Maglie and Jones.

But this is not about Todd Jones the pitcher. It's about Todd Jones the columnist. These days, most athletes retire to become instant television analysts. Jones has gone in another direction. He writes a column for the Detroit Free Press and The Sporting News.

Other players have become writers — most of them after retirement. Only a few have written while active.

One was Early Wynn. When he pitched for the Indians, Early wrote a column for the Cleveland News. His job suddenly ended when Cleveland traded him to the White Sox after he had berated the front office for trying to trade him.

Today, Todd Jones is the only active big leaguer with a column.

Jones has been a columnist since 1993, when he broke into the big leagues with Houston. "I had no classes, no training in writing," he said, "but in the off-season, I called the Anniston (Ala.) Star, and they gave me a column assignment. After that, the Birmingham News published me for 11 straight years."

Jones wrote his early columns in longhand and mailed them to the Star. However, for the News he had to learn to type. Todd's work also has appeared in the Houston Chronicle, and he did a weekly column for the Palm Beach Post while pitching for the Florida Marlins in 2005.

"I usually write on the plane, when we have some downtime," Jones said. "I enjoy telling about players' personalities. A lot of people want to tie a player to the stats on the back of his baseball card. I go for the personal perspective.

"For example, Curtis Granderson buys his shoes at Wal-Mart. Joel Zumaya got four new tattoos in spring training. Jason Grilli wears the number his dad wore, 49. Jose Mesa always had that same number, but when he joined the Tigers, he deferred to Grilli and switched to 94."

I asked Todd what his wife, Michelle, thought about his column. "She enjoys it," he said. "She wrote a column herself last fall for The Sporting News and got lot more response than I ever had."

And what about the players, how do they react?

"They've been great," Todd said. "Nobody has ever said anything bad about my column. They seem to like it. Managers and coaches, too. I try to be protective toward them. I'm very conscious of not talking out of school and encroaching on their privacy. It's a job I enjoy, and I want to keep doing it."

ORIGINALLY PRINTED APRIL 30, 2007.

ERNIE HARWELL

Bonds deserves the recognition

Now that Barry Bonds has hit his record-breaking home run, he deserves to be recognized as the new home run king — without reservation. Commissioner Bud Selig owed it to Bonds to be there to honor him.

I realize Bonds has many detractors because of his negative personality and alleged involvement with steroids. His personality should not be a factor when we talk about baseball records.

As for steroids and other drugs, the evidence against Bonds remains fuzzy. Many players in the 1990s probably used steroids and other enhancers. Some of these drugs were legal, some weren't. I don't think anyone will prove who took drugs and who didn't.

Baseball historians probably will look at this era and conclude that Bonds was one of many who hurt baseball with drug involvement. And Bonds' home run record will remain official and in the record books until the next slugger comes along to surpass it.

ORIGINALLY PRINTED AUG. 9, 2007.

OH, THE MEMORIES

 ERNIE ON HIS LAST TIGER STADIUM BROADCAST:
To me it will always be The Corner, the most famous corner in Michigan. Tiger Stadium has been a dear friend. ... The Corner is part of our history, our heritage, it has been magic, hope and a true heartbeat of our city. 99

DISC 3, ERNIE HARWELL'S AUDIO SCRAPBOOK

Ewbank a legendary coach and friend

Although baseball is my favorite sport, I was first a football announcer. In 1956 — midway in that phase of my career — I worked with a great coach and an even greater person, Weeb Ewbank.

Ewbank was developing the Baltimore Colts into champions. Soon, John Unitas, Raymond Berry and Don Shula would enhance their reputations through the genius of Ewbank. Meanwhile, Ewbank would prove to me that he could not only be a master of football but also a true friend. His football record is public knowledge. His talent for lasting friendship is a quality shared by only a few privileged associates.

In the mid-1950s, NFL coaches didn't have much appreciation for their play-by-play announcers. We were merely tolerated by most, but Ewbank was different. He went beyond token cooperation.

"Would you like to have a copy of our Colts playbook?" he asked me one fall afternoon. I was overwhelmed by his offer. Most coaches were more secretive than the CIA, but here was my chance to study the same arcane details of Colts football that only the insiders were allowed to view.

Ewbank also lent me game films of the opponents. I could sit in my basement and study the movies over and over. This enabled me to learn the mannerisms and tendencies of the players — a tremendous help for any broadcaster. We didn't have videos in those days, and coaches wouldn't dare share films with anybody.

There was another way Ewbank helped. On the eve of a game, he would tell me the first offensive play he planned to use.

"My first play," he would say, "will be a quick over-the-middle pass." So, I would enter a broadcast with knowledge of the game's beginning. It gave me added confidence.

Away from the field, Ewbank was warm and caring. He and his wife, Lucy, often visited our home in Baltimore. I remember one evening we invited them for dinner, along with Milton Eisenhower, who lived next door. Milton was the president of Johns Hopkins University and brother of President Dwight Eisenhower. Ewbank and Milton got along great. Eisenhower wanted to talk football, and Ewbank kept probing Milton about politics. Meanwhile, Lucy became interested in learning to play the electric organ and later decided to take lessons. It was fun that night as we all enjoyed my wife Lulu's tasty dinner and the enlightening conversation.

I look back with fondness on those days. Ewbank, who was 91 when he died in 1998, established himself as a coaching giant, a member of the Pro Football Hall of Fame. But I remember him best as a true friend who cared about everybody — even his play-by-play announcer.

ORIGINALLY PRINTED AUG. 16, 2004.

Returning to D.C. a capital idea

Welcome back, Washington. Our nation's capital is returning to Major League Baseball. My first brush with baseball in Washington came in the spring of 1945 when I was in the Marines, preparing to go overseas. As sports editor of the Marine magazine, Leatherneck, I visited the Senators' wartime spring training camp in nearby College Park, Md., to write an article about Bert Shepard, a war hero trying out with the team. His plane had been shot down over Germany, and he had lost his right leg. With an artificial leg, Bert was struggling to make the team. He hung on and eventually pitched one game for the 1945 Senators.

It wasn't until 1954 that I returned to Washington, broadcasting for the Orioles. It was an easy trip. We could drive the 30 miles ourselves or take the team bus. Another option was to spend the night in a Washington hotel or return to Baltimore after each game.

I have vivid memories of Washington's Griffith Stadium. I am fond of figs, and there was a fig tree in front of the ballpark. I was probably the only guy who ate those figs.

At the front gate of the stadium was a two-story stucco house. Downstairs was a modest ticket office, and on the second floor owner Clark Griffith kept his office, the site of his daily pinochle game with old cronies. Despite his reputation as a penny-pincher, he was kind, gentle and generous. To improve his meager attendance, he would schedule a doubleheader with the flimsiest of excuses.

One afternoon our Orioles bus arrived at Griffith Stadium for a night game, only to discover it had been postponed. The skies were clear. But Griff had called the game because of rain to set up a double-header the next night. On the bus back to Baltimore, Orioles manager Paul Richards said, "Somebody spits out of the window, so Griff calls the game."

Opening Day was always special at Griffith Stadium — and later at RFK Stadium — because the president usually threw out the first ball. In 1955, I wrote an article for Parade magazine about that custom. My lead said President Dwight Eisenhower would throw out the ceremonial first pitch. The magazine was printed a week or so before the event. But Ike decided he would skip the opener and go to Augusta, Ga., for the Masters.

With the magazine already printed, Jesse Gorkin, Parade's editor, faced a huge problem. He asked me to get Griff to urge the president to follow his origi-nal plan. Griff tried, but Ike optioned for golf. Each paper with the Parade article had to print an apolo-gy on its front page, explaining the snafu.

But the incident ended with an ironic twist. Ike went to Augusta, but the baseball opener was rained out. The president returned to Washington and threw out the first pitch for the rescheduled opener.

ORIGINALLY PRINTED APRIL 4, 2005.

We'll miss Casey at the mike

J ust before the start of the 2005 baseball season, Bob Casey, the only public-address announcer in Minnesota Twins history, died. The Metrodome will never be the same.

No stadium ever had a more authoritative voice. Casey, 79, was like a maitre d' who dominates a fancy restaurant or the unyielding doorman at a deluxe Manhattan apartment. Casey and his voice let everybody in the ballpark know who was boss.

There was nothing coaxing or diplomatic about Casey's delivery. He came straight to the point. Sometimes he butchered the language. Often he stumbled over names. To Casey, polish was for shoes — not for pronouncements.

Some of his vocal slipups became legendary. The best known happened at Metropolitan Stadium in the 1970s. It is Paul Carey's favorite memory of the fabled PA man.

The police had received a bomb threat.

"We are going to evacuate the stadium," they told Casey. "But we urge you to be very careful about how you make this announcement. It is most important that you word it so that we can avoid any panic whatsoever. All we ask you to do is to request that everybody in the stadium to leave in a most orderly fashion."

Casey gave it his best, most reassuring treatment. "Attention, attention, ladies and gentlemen, do not panic," he intoned. "The police have informed the Twins that there will be an explosion here in the stadium within the next 15 minutes."

The startled crowd — and even some players — hurried out of the ballpark.

Casey's stiffest test always came in September, when clubs expanded their rosters, bringing up unknown rookies. One of these was Don Pepper, a young Tigers first baseman. In the late innings in 1966, Pepper entered a game as a pinch-hitter. He was a complete unknown to Casey, who had access to only his number and last name. The crusty PA man quickly improvised. "Now pinch-hitting for Detroit," he announced, "Salty Pepper."

After that, every time I would meet Casey at the ballpark, I would always rag him about his quick, off-the-cuff invention of a first name for Don Pepper.

ORIGINALLY PRINTED APRIL 11, 2005.

Holidays, baseball rarely mix now

What happened to the Fourth of July? I know there were auto trips, picnics and fireworks. But I'm thinking about the Fourth of July and baseball.

The Fourth was once a significant time in baseball, marking the halfway point of a pennant race. All kinds of stats about the Fourth would pack the sports pages. Experts would tell us what percentage of teams leading the league on that date eventually won the pennant. Or we would read the history of comebacks. The favorite reference was always the Boston Braves dashing from last place on July 4, 1914, to the National League pennant.

Individual averages were measured the same way — before and after the Fourth. Now, the All-Star break is the measurement.

The baseball season used to have five milestones — Opening Day, Memorial Day, Fourth of July, Labor Day and the final day of the season. Opening Day was the new beginning. Everybody starting even. By Memorial Day, fans had seen enough games to get an early feel about the pennant race. Fourth of July meant the halfway point, a sort of catch-your-breath-and-get-ready-for-the-remainder-of-the-season rest stop. Labor Day marked the beginning of the stretch drive, when the race belonged to the surviving few. Then came the final game and the crowning of a pennant winner.

In the old days, Memorial Day, the Fourth of July and Labor Day meant doubleheaders. Fourth of July was extra special. Before the easy access to freeways, excursion trains would bring thousands of fans to city stadiums. Special events testing various skills of the players would enhance the afternoon's enjoyment. There would be relays, racing around the bases, throwing contests for outfielders and catchers competing with throws through a barrel at second base. It was all part of the Fourth of July tradition.

Now on the Fourth, there are no more scheduled doubleheaders, except a possibility of a makeup game added to a regularly scheduled game. These day/night twin bills are billed as a doubleheader, but they are not recognized as such in statistical records. The record book says these are two single games with separate admissions.

I miss the special meaning of this once special day. I saw my very first game July 4, 1926, at Ponce de Leon Park in Atlanta. I don't remember much about that minor league doubleheader except that Eddie Morgan of the New Orleans Pelicans hit a home run. Since then, I've seen a few more games — some of them Fourth of July doubleheaders, a great tradition now long gone.

ORIGINALLY PRINTED JULY 5, 2005.

When the playoffs weren't the thing

T he playoffs have become such a huge media blast, it's hard to believe how insignificant they were in their first year, 1969.

The radio industry didn't consider the National League playoffs important enough to put them on a national network. But Bud Blattner and I broadcast the first American League Championship Series between Baltimore and Minnesota. It was on a coast-to-coast network set up by Robert Wold Co., a forerunner of ESPN.

The Tigers' 1968 World Series triumph had climaxed the last pure baseball season, when each league consisted of 10 clubs and the winners met for the championship. Along came expansion with its playoff system.

The three-game series began in the afternoon, Oct. 4, at Baltimore's Memorial Stadium. The stadium was far from being filled. Blattner and I didn't even have a booth. We worked surrounded by fans in the leftfield upper deck.

The first two games were close and exciting. The Orioles won the opener in the 12th inning, 4-3, on Paul Blair's two-out suicide squeeze.

In the second game, the Birds took another thriller. Dave McNally pitched an 11-inning, 1-0 victory. A two-out, pinch-hit single by Curt Motton won it.

The series moved to Minnesota's Metropolitan Stadium, and Baltimore crushed the Twins, 11-2, to complete a sweep. Orioles pitchers declawed Rod Carew, who had won the first of his seven batting titles. He had only a single in 14 at-bats.

In those days, baseball didn't have its modern, two-tiered playoff plan. So Baltimore advanced directly to the World Series, losing to the Miracle Mets in five games.

After that first playoff broadcast, there was no definite radio pattern until 1976, when CBS began to cover both leagues.

I worked the first CBS AL broadcast with Ned Martin, the Red Sox announcer. I did playoffs each year for CBS, except in 1984 and 1987, when I was on the Tigers' network.

When ESPN replaced CBS, I continued on the playoffs and enjoyed every game. Of course, my favorite playoff memories involved the Tigers.

From small beginnings, the playoffs have increased in importance to a point where they encroach on World Series interest. The listener (or viewer) hears so many facts in those 12 (or fewer) postseason games that by World Series time the endless minutiae is mind-numbing.

Also, the playoffs have a sudden-death appeal that enhances their drama. If you don't win, you go home. In the World Series, even if a team loses, there's still consolation of a pennant won and a showcase in the Series.

I believe the playoffs involve too many games. But, I realize, baseball prefers as many games as it can sell to TV and to the public.

Ideally, I'd like to see the first round be best of three. Or maybe just one game — sudden death. Then, best of five in the championship series. Thus, the best-of-seven World Series would regain some of its lost luster.

It'll never happen, but it is still fun to speculate about the possibility.

ORIGINALLY PRINTED OCT. 3, 2006.

Commish gave Tigers homefield in '35

Because the American League won the 2006 All-Star Game, the World Series opened in Detroit, then moved to St. Louis.

Until the All-Star-winner rule was adopted, the leagues alternated the site of the Series opener each year.

An exception happened in the 1935 classic between the Tigers and the Chicago Cubs. The Cubs won 21 straight games at the end of the season to become a surprise National League pennant winner. However, the club's front office had neither time nor manpower to deal with the demand for tickets and other last-minute problems.

So commissioner Kenesaw Mountain Landis moved the opener from Chicago to Detroit. Because the Tigers had opened the 1934 Series against the Cardinals at Navin Field, the 1935 switch gave Detroit the first two games at home for two straight years.

The Detroiters lost the '34 series to the Cards in seven games. But in '35, they beat the Cubs in six games for their first World Series title.

ORIGINALLY PRINTED OCT. 24, 2006.

1911 Series delayed by rain, dinner dates

Think rain was a problem in the 2006 World Series? Check out 1911. Action between the Philadelphia A's and the New York Giants was delayed a whole week by rain. One game was postponed not by baseball bosses, but by a sports writer named Hugh Fullerton.

Before Game 4, Fullerton was in New York, hoping to keep a dinner date and wondering if rain would wash out the game in Philly. He decided to visit the hotel room of American League president Ban Johnson, who had authority to postpone the game.

Through an open door, Fullerton heard the phone ring. He quickly answered. It was Johnson's secretary. "Shall I call it?" the secretary asked, thinking he was talking to his boss. "Rain has stopped here in Philly, but the ground is wet and soggy."

Fullerton said, "Call it off."

Walking down the hall, Fullerton met Johnson.

"I called the game," he told Johnson, not explaining that he did it because of his New York dinner date.

"That's fine," Johnson said. "I had a special date here in New York anyway."

ORIGINALLY PRINTED OCT. 28, 2006.

All-Star Game more than one-day event

The All-Star Game started as a one-time-only event. Now — 75 years later — it is the best and longest-running All-Star Game of all major sports.

In the midst of the Great Depression, most owners opposed the game. They feared it would cut into their gate receipts and that some of their star players might be injured.

The All-Star idea wasn't exactly new. In 1858, the best players from various Brooklyn teams met stars from New York nines. Around 1910, the Baseball Magazine began to campaign for an All-Star Game. In 1933, it became a reality, thanks to the efforts of Arch Ward, sports editor of the Chicago Tribune and sports chairman of the Chicago World's Fair. Ward used his influence with baseball commissioner Kenesaw Mountain Landis to establish his idea.

After the first game, the National League asked for a rematch. Several years later, the National League brass wanted to discontinue the event because the American League had won the first five meetings. At that point the game, growing in popularity, had ingrained itself as a vital part of the season.

Today, baseball's All-Star Game is one of the jew-

ROMAIN BLANQUART

The All-Star Game visited Comerica Park in 2005. What started as a one-time event has become a jewel of the sports year.

els of the sports year. It has become more than just a one-day event. The game remains a centerpiece but has lost its impact because of surrounding attractions. For instance, the Home Run Derby has taken some of the shine off the big game.

Also, the game has less glamour than it possessed in pre-TV times. In those days, fans seldom saw players of the other league in action. In an

American League town, it was an exciting novelty to watch the National Leaguers in All-Star action. Not anymore. Any day or night, the TV watcher can see players of both leagues on the tube. The novelty is gone.

Nevertheless, baseball has the best of all All-Star Games. Players play hard and play to win. And the rules don't differ from the rules of the regular season, as they do in other sports.

Yes, the game started as a one-time event, but it is certainly here to stay.

ORIGINALLY PRINTED JULY 9, 2007.

PURELY PERSONAL

 ERNIE ON BEING FIRED BY THE TIGERS IN 1990:
Quite a few (Hall of Fame announcers) have been fired. ... I never held any bitterness or acrimony about that. ... I think it was probably the best thing in the long run that every happened in my career. **99**

DISC 3, ERNIE HARWELL'S AUDIO SCRAPBOOK

Cobb telegraphed early exploits

This is a baseball column, but the setting is the 1941 Masters. It was the first golf tournament I broadcast, and it brought me together with two boyhood heroes.

What a thrill! I was in the locker room in Augusta, Ga., with Ty Cobb, the Georgia Peach, and Grantland Rice, the revered king of sports writing.

I had met both before but only briefly. I did a radio interview the year before with Cobb in his hometown of Royston, Ga. And at age 9 or 10, I delivered my mother's biscuits to Rice in his railroad car, which took him through Atlanta to New York after spring training.

In Augusta, Rice was talking to Cobb and a small group of writers. "Ty, a lot of people give me credit for discovering you," Rice said. "I was sports editor of the Atlanta Journal when you were playing in Anniston, Ala., in 1904."

"Yeah," Cobb said. "I remember. That was a tough time for me."

"Almost every day," Rice continued, "I'd get a telegram about you, all of them describing your play in glowing terms. It would be: 'Cobb was brilliant today with two doubles and a triple.' Or 'Cobb stars again with three steals and a home run.' Or 'Young Cobb runs wild as Anniston wins.' Those telegrams just kept coming.

"I began to mention you in my columns, but I still hadn't seen you in action. When I finally saw you, you were just as good as those telegrams had touted."

Cobb broke into the conversation. "Yeah, Granny, I remember when you and I met that year. It was the first time I'd ever been interviewed by a newspaper man. Even then, you had a great reputation, and I was in awe of you."

Rice said: "We've known each other a long time. I've followed your career every step of the way. What a great career it was. We've been friends a long time, Ty, and I'm proud to be the guy who discovered you. And Ty, it all started with those glowing telegrams about your exploits in Anniston."

Cobb reached over and put his hand on Rice's knee. "Granny," he said. "Do you know who sent those telegrams?"

"No, I don't," Rice said.

"It was me, Granny," Cobb said. "I sent them to you."

ORIGINALLY PRINTED APRIL 5, 2004.

Series rings should be for select few

The Boston Red Sox got it all wrong when they distributed their 2004 World Series rings.
These rings were won on the playing field and should be awarded only to the players and a few others close to the team.

The Red Sox gave hundreds of rings — to scouts, front-office personnel and minority owners of the team. These owners included executives of the New York Times and the Boston Globe.

The Tigers gave me World Series rings in 1968 and 1984. I deeply appreciated the gesture but realized I didn't deserve them. Usually a team rewards its groundskeeper, equipment manager, traveling secretary and a few others. It should stop there. I don't remember who else received rings in '68, but I do recall that after the 1984 triumph, owner Tom Monaghan distributed rings to all the front-office people and many of the executives of his Domino's Pizza company.

Remember the case of Bill Scherrer's ring? Bill was a skinny left-handed pitcher who joined the Tigers from Cincinnati during the '84 season. He relieved in 18 games and had a 1-0 record in 19 innings. Though he didn't pitch against Kansas City in the American League playoffs, Scherrer appeared in three World Series games against San

---

Diego.

Some of the Tigers' World Series rings were of much better quality than others. Scherrer's ring was an inferior one — the same kind given to many of the pizza people. A jeweler's appraisal confirmed Scherrer's fears. Scherrer protested to management, but nobody listened.

ORIGINALLY PRINTED APRIL 25, 2005.

Best stories often come from elders

A year before he died, Cardinals announcer Jack Buck and I were chatting behind the batting cage at Busch Stadium in St. Louis. "Ernie," he said, "there's only one thing good about you. You'll never die young."

He was right. And now I have become an expert on something for the first time in my life — old age.

When I think of old age in baseball, I think of four people — Elden Auker, Satchel Paige, Rick Ferrell and Connie Mack.

A few years ago, when Elden and Tommy Lasorda were taking a 2 1/2-hour drive from Vero Beach to the Ted Williams museum in Hernando, Fla., Auker did all the driving and the much-younger Lasorda did all the sleeping.

Although I interviewed him several times, I was never close with Paige. He was the symbol of age in baseball. Nobody knew his true age, but we all knew he was old.

And his famous quotation, "Don't look back, someone might be gaining on you," will last forever. Satch is one of the few baseball people listed in Bartlett's Familiar Quotations.

Ferrell was close to 90 and still working when I thought he had the best job in the world. His good friend, Jim Campbell, made Rick a Tigers vice

GABRIEL B. TAIT

Elden Auker, a true gentleman shown here in 1999, was a member of the 1935 champion Tigers and played golf with Babe Ruth.

president and consultant with a lavish office.

Ferrell would come in about 11 a.m., eat lunch, take a nap and go home. He was a wonderful friend, always kind and considerate, and a most capable executive.

Mack was a major league catcher in the 1880s, then managed for a record 53 years. He was 93 when he died in 1956.

I first interviewed him in Atlanta at the 1940 National Baseball Convention. He sparkled with

keen insights about Rube Waddell and other stars
he had managed in the early 1900s.

In the final year of his life, Mack came to
Baltimore for a ceremony honoring one of his great
players, Frank (Home Run) Baker.

I was to emcee that on-the-field tribute. The
Orioles brass warned me not to allow Mack to
speak. Because he had lost his mental sharpness,
they were afraid what he might say. When I introduced him, he somehow seized the mike from me,
launching into rambling gibberish. I couldn't stop
him. When he finally wound down, I continued the
ceremonies.

I couldn't help but contrast Mack's performance
with our 1941 interview, when he was so sharp at
the age of 79. But how can you criticize a 93-year-
old guy who won more games than any other manager in baseball history?

ORIGINALLY PRINTED MAY 2, 2005.

Some quotes stand the test of time

Since the first stone toss in the Caveman Olympics, quotes have been a part of sports. Through the years, I've collected baseball quotes, and I hereby submit a few samples. Some might even be true.

When Joe DiMaggio was a rookie with the Yankees, a reporter asked him for a quote. Later in his career, Joe said, "I was so naïve that I thought he was talking about a soft drink."

Hall of Famer Satchel Paige's advice to a young pitcher: "Throw strikes. The plate don't move."

Mick Kelleher, light-hitting Tigers infielder: "What's one home run? If you hit one, they're just going to want you to hit two."

When ex-Tigers manager Ralph Houk managed Triple-A Denver, he delivered these guarded words during an argument with an umpire: "I thought you'd like to know that on my way to the ballpark, I passed a kennel, and your mother is all right."

Bob Cerv, a strong Kansas City slugger but mediocre outfielder, suffered a broken jaw and had it wired back in place. When Cerv dropped an easy fly in Yankee Stadium, a reporter wrote: "They should have wired his glove instead of his jaw."

Hitting slumps seem to be the most popular source for quotes. Vance Law, a Cubs infielder, once said, "When you're in a slump, you look out at the field and it's a great big glove."

Terry Kennedy, San Diego catcher, had this statement on the topic: "A slump is like the common cold. It lasts two weeks no matter what you do."

When asked what a player needs most while in a slump, Yankees manager Miller Huggins said, "A good string of alibis."

Tigers first-base coach Andy Van Slyke was an outstanding outfielder and hitting star with the Cardinals and Pirates. Bedeviled by a batting slump, Andy said, "I'm so bad, I couldn't even drive Miss Daisy home."

Why did light-hitting Ernie Fazio of the old Houston Colt 45s switch from a 33-ounce bat to 29 ounces? "After I strike out, the 29-ounce bat is much easier to carry back to the dugout."

In 1935, Cubs manager Charlie Grimm had a running feud with a Chicago writer. Win or lose, he was the constant target of the reporter's heavy criticism. After the Cubs had won 21 straight games, they lost one. The writer said to Grimm, "I knew you couldn't keep it up."

Answering the question of how to pitch to Yankees slugger Mickey Mantle, Frank Sullivan of the Red Sox said, "With tears in my eyes."

Looking at an unflattering picture of himself, Mets pitcher Jeff Innis said, "This photograph was taken out of context."

Here's a quote about quotes from the most quoted, Yogi Berra, who once was quoted as saying, "I didn't say anything I said."

ORIGINALLY PRINTED JULY 31, 2006.

Red-hot history of a ballpark favorite

t was David Letterman who said: "I love baseball. I love the horsehide, I love the rosin, I love the pine tar — and that's just in the hot dogs."

That first bite on Opening Day started a big summer for the hot dog.

Hot dog-eating contests have made headlines. And Comerica Park's singing hot dog man, Charley Marcuse, won a national competition.

With the help of my neighbor, Mike Chirio, I discovered hot dog history on Linda Stradley's Web site, www.whatscookingamerica.net.

As a kid, I loved hot dogs. (In Georgia we called them weenies.) Once I became a baseball announcer and they were so available, I vowed not to eat them. If I started, I'd have no restraint and end up weighing 500 pounds. I made one exception: At Milwaukee's County Stadium, I allowed myself one bratwurst per game.

Here are some facts about the hot dog. In one year, Americans eat an average of 60 apiece — most of them between Memorial Day and Labor Day.

Sausage is one of the oldest forms of processed food. It dates to the Ninth Century B.C., with a mention in Homer's Odyssey.

Five years before Columbus sailed to America, the frankfurter was developed in Frankfurt,

GABRIEL B. TAIT

Charley Marcuse, Comerica Park's famed singing hot dog man, patrols the park's lower bowl just about every Tigers game.

Germany.

Folks in Vienna, Austria, point to the term "wiener" to prove their city is the birthplace of the hot dog.

But the frankfurter and wiener don't become hot dogs until put into a bun or roll. Who did this first? It's a mystery.

Here's the version I like: The term "hot dog" was coined in 1902 during a New York Giants game at the Polo Grounds.

On a cold, rainy afternoon, concessionaire Harry M. Stevens couldn't sell ice cream. He rounded up all the sausages he could find and put them into rolls. Vendors shouted, "They're red hot. Get your sausages while they're hot."

In the press box that afternoon, cartoonist Ted Dorgan was desperate for an idea. When he heard the vendors, he quickly drew a cartoon of a frankfurter with a tail, legs and head.

It looked like a dachshund. Not sure how to spell "dachshund," he simply wrote "hot dog." The cartoon was a sensation, and the term "hot dog" was born.

I prefer this version, because when I broadcast for the Brooklyn Dodgers in the late '40s, I often ate lunch with the son of the hot dog originator, Harry Stevens, in his Ebbets Field office. Believe me, we didn't eat hot dogs.

The lowly hot dog's shining moment came June 11, 1939, at Hyde Park, N.Y. President and Mrs. Franklin D. Roosevelt entertained King George VI of England and the Queen.

They served hot dogs to the royal guests. The King was so pleased that he asked Mrs. Roosevelt for another.

My favorite hot dog quote is from Lawrence J. Peter: "The noblest of all dogs is the hot dog. It feeds the hand that bites it."

ORIGINALLY PRINTED AUG. 28, 2006.

THE CLOSER

> **ERNIE ON SIGNING OFF HIS LAST GAME IN 2002:**
> Thank you for taking me with you to that cottage Up North, to the beach, the picnic, your work place and your backyard. Thank you for sneaking your transistor radio under the pillow as you grew up loving the Tigers.

DISC 4, ERNIE HARWELL'S AUDIO SCRAPBOOK

Angels lend a hand

D o you believe in angels? I do. Three times in my travels these messengers from God have helped me reach my goals.

In my first year of broadcasting for the Baltimore Orioles in 1954, my family lived 30 miles south of the city. My wife, Lulu, drove me to the Pennsylvania Station in Baltimore so I could catch the afternoon train to Philadelphia, where the Orioles were playing a night game against the A's. After I had said goodbye to Lulu, she drove away. It was then I realized I had no money or credit cards.

I went to the ticket window to explain my problem.

"I'm the new Oriole announcer," I told the ticket seller. "I must get to Philly for my broadcast, and I have no way to buy a ticket."

"That's all right," he said. "I will pay for your ticket and also lend you $10. You can pay whenever you return to the station."

My next angel appeared in Hollywood, Calif., during the All-Star break in July 1978. The Tigers' final game before the break was Sunday night in Texas. Their next one was Thursday in Seattle. In those days I was active in songwriting. It made no sense to go home during the break. So I flew from Texas to Seattle, with a stopover in Hollywood to peddle my songs.

After a day with singers, producers and record executives, I had a quiet dinner and a good night's sleep at the Roosevelt Hotel and was up early the next day to catch my plane.

I got on the airport bus and settled into my seat. After riding three blocks, I realized my briefcase was missing. It contained my songs, wallet, driver's license and credit cards. When we stopped to pick up passengers at the next hotel, I spoke to the driver.

"Will you please check your luggage bin to see if my briefcase is there?" I asked.

He looked but couldn't find it.

"Maybe I left it at the Roosevelt. Can you drive back there?"

"No. I'm not allowed to," he said.

"Please, it's very important to me."

"All right," he said. "But go back to your seat and don't say anything."

He drove the bus to the Roosevelt. I ran into the lobby. There, leaning against a post, was my briefcase.

My third angel encounter happened in 2001 on the way to the Oakland-Pontiac airport. The Tigers were flying to New York on Redbird II. I made a wrong turn and was lost. Traveling a strange road with only 15 minutes until departure, I began to panic.

I pulled off the road, where three men were working on a truck.

"I'm lost," I said. "Can you tell me how to find the Pontiac airport?"

"Don't worry," one of them said. "Follow me."

He jumped into his truck and led me all the way to the airport. I made it just in time.

ORIGINALLY PRINTED AUG. 9, 2004.

EXTRA INNINGS

ERNIE ON BASEBALL: Baseball is a tongue-tied kid from Georgia growing up to be an announcer and praising the Lord for showing him the way to Cooperstown.

DISC 4, ERNIE HARWELL'S AUDIO SCRAPBOOK

Ernie returns to the airwaves

Ernie Harwell began his career in radio and television in 1940 and signed off after the 2002 Tigers season.

"I'm not leaving, folks," he told his listeners after his final Tigers broadcast Sept. 29, 2002. "I'll still be with you."

Indeed, retirement hasn't stopped him from making several returns to the broadcast booth for special occasions and guest appearances.

At the 2005 All-Star Game in Detroit, he joined the Fox telecast during a pregame ceremony and even called one at-bat in the fourth inning for ESPN radio.

During the Tigers' 2006 American League Division Series against the Yankees, he joined the ESPN telecast for two innings of Game 3 at Comerica Park. He spent the third and fourth innings with ESPN's Jon Miller and Joe Morgan. Harwell even used his trademark "house-by-the-side-of-the-road" line and "excessive window shopping" comment on two called third strikes.

During the 2006 World Series between the Tigers and Cardinals, Harwell broadcast the second inning of Game 1 on the Tigers' radio network, alongside former partners Dan Dickerson and Jim Price.

AMY LEANG

Inside Comerica Park is a statue of Ernie Harwell. "What a thrill!" Harwell said when the statue was unveiled in 2002.

Harwell made more appearances during the 2007 Tigers season. He joined the ESPN Sunday night crew for two innings of a 1-0 victory over the Twins on July 1 and worked two games for FSN Detroit as a fill-in for Rod Allen, who was attending his son's high school graduation. Harwell also subbed for Allen in 2003.

Free Press sports writers Mike Brudenell, George Sipple, Mark Snyder, Jo-Ann Barnas and John Lowe chronicle some of Harwell's returns to the booth in the pages that follow.

Grand night for Ernie, Detroit

BY MIKE BRUDENELL

Take a bow, Ernie. Take a bow, Detroit. On a balmy evening when Tigers broadcasting legend Ernie Harwell returned to the microphone to call one at-bat in the 2005 All-Star Game, the Motor City put on a show that was gracious and spectacular.

The Fox telecast opened with colorful shots from around the city, from Motown singers to automobile factories. Before the game at Comerica Park, the Detroit Symphony Orchestra played "God Save the Queen" out of respect for those killed in the terrorist attacks in London. A stealth bomber flew low over the stadium to the sound of the national anthem.

The 41,000-plus in attendance at Detroit's first All-Star Game since 1971 bowed their heads for a moment in silence, then cheered roundly. The feel-good night buried the memories of the 1984 World Series aftermath and its overturned cars and gunfire.

During the pregame ceremony, Fox Sports hosts Kevin Kennedy and Jeanne Zelasko introduced Harwell, dressed in a dark jacket and his signature

JULIAN H. GONZALEZ

Ernie Harwell greets former Dodgers manager Tommy Lasorda before the 2005 All-Star Game. Harwell called one at-bat for Fox.

hat, to the national TV audience.

As darkness fell over the city, Fox cameras located Harwell's statue near the entrance to Comerica Park. Play-by-play announcer Joe Buck paid tribute to Harwell.

"Ernie Harwell is beloved in this city," Buck said. "You will never meet a better baseball man."

On ESPN radio, Harwell talked at length as he prepared to call an at-bat in the fourth inning. Asked about the standing ovation from the crowd as he walked on the field before the game, Harwell replied:

"It made me feel great. It was a warm, fuzzy feeling."

Pressed about being a baseball broadcaster, 55 years in the majors, Harwell said in typical modest fashion:

"I started out hoping I could do it in the minor leagues. I never thought I would last seven decades. I love this game."

In 1971, Harwell watched the All-Star Game at Tiger Stadium as a spectator. He recalled Reggie Jackson's mammoth home run that year.

"Everyone loved Jackson's homer," Harwell said. "I think it is still going in outer space."

With Livan Hernandez pitching in the bottom of the fourth to Jason Varitek, a confident Harwell went to work. When Hernandez walked the batter, Harwell turned it back over to the ESPN radio crew.

"That was a pretty exciting time I had with you guys," Harwell joked. "Thanks for letting me butt in here."

As Harwell left the broadcast booth as the inning ended, he said: "Thank you, guys. Come back and see us."

That was Detroit's message to baseball fans across America. Come back, we enjoyed having you.

ORIGINALLY PRINTED JULY 13, 2005.

Harwell recalls All-Star broadcasts

BY MIKE BRUDENELL

Ernie Harwell, whose major league broadcasting career began in 1948, never called an All-Star Game in Detroit until 2005. Speaking with the Free Press, he reflected on the previous games played in the Motor City:

1941

"They didn't have TV coverage, just radio. The Mutual network broadcast the game nationally. Red Barber, Bob Elson, Mel Allen and France Laux were the announcers. Red was a great reporter who was accurate and precise. Allen was enthusiastic and had a great voice. He was identified with the New York Yankees. Elson was a veteran announcer from Chicago who started in the '20s. He broadcast White Sox and Cubs games. Laux was from St. Louis."

Also in 1941

Ty Tyson, the Tigers' first announcer, handled the game for local radio station WWJ. "Tyson lived in Grosse Pointe," Harwell said. "He had a wry sense of humor. He was a great guy. After he retired, I'd take him to baseball games."

1951

"They showed the game on NBC-TV and broadcast it on the Mutual network. The radio announcers were Mel Allen and Al Helfer, who was Mutual's sports guy. Jack Brickhouse and Jim Britt handled TV. Jack was a Chicago announcer, and Britt worked in Boston."

1971

"NBC Radio and NBC-TV covered the All-Star Game in Detroit. Jim Simpson and Sandy Koufax did radio, while Curt Gowdy and Tony Kubek were the TV guys. I was purely a spectator. I sat up in the third deck near the rightfield foul line. There was a little breeze blowing. It was a beautiful night. It was a terrific game. I was very relaxed. Reggie Jackson was tremendous. His home run hit the transformer."

ORIGINALLY PRINTED JULY 11, 2005.

A wanted man in Detroit

BY GEORGE SIPPLE

Ernie Harwell talked to the Free Press about a variety of topics surrounding the 2005 All-Star Game and why he's so involved.

QUESTION: How does the current All-Star Game and its related events compare with the past All-Star Games held here?

ANSWER: Now it's so much more than it used to be. Now it's a spectacle that lasts a week. It gets the fans involved, which I think is great.

Q: Why are you working so much instead of just taking in the events?

A: I enjoy working. That's part of my persona. I don't want to sit in the corner and do nothing.

Q: What do you think of the Home Run Derby?

A: I think it's fun. I don't think it takes away from the game. I think the fans are interested in comparing sluggers from one team against another, one league against another, one country against another.

Q: And what do you think of being in the radio booth again?

A: I love that. I think it's great. I really felt flattered by that. I know how it is with visitors in the booth. I sometimes feel like I'm encroaching a little bit, but if they set it up, it's fine with me.

Q: Were there extra events surrounding the 1971 All-Star Game?

A: The only thing I can remember that was extracurricular was the commissioner had a luncheon at the Book Cadillac. I was the emcee. I don't remember much about it; maybe the commissioner gave some sort of talk.

Q: Are there any players you're looking forward to seeing?

A: I love Ichiro (Suzuki). He's one of my favorites. I hope he gets to play. He's a reserve. I look forward to seeing some of the National Leaguers. There's some great players in the National League.

Q: What do you make of the selection of Ivan Rodriguez?

A: I think he's probably the most representative guy the Tigers could have. He's better known outside the city than anyone else.

Q: What do you think about Jeremy Bonderman and Brandon Inge not making it?

A: It would have been nice for them to go, but I can understand (Terry) Francona's take on that. I think Bonderman's going to have a lot of times to pitch. Inge is sort of the victim. I think all through All-Star history we've had guys who had great first halves who weren't selected. It's just something you sort of have to accept.

ORIGINALLY PRINTED JULY 11, 2005.

An old friend returns for playoff baseball

BY MARK SNYDER

Yankees outfielder Hideki Matsui stood at home plate in the second inning of Game 3 of the 2006 American League Division Series, watching Tigers left-hander Kenny Rogers' called third strike.

Then the voice — the only voice most Tigers fans recall with a playoff team — followed with a catchphrase dearly missed: "He stood there like the house by the side of the road and watched that one go by."

Ernie Harwell, whose statue greets visitors at Comerica Park, was back in the broadcast booth at times during Game 3, his first extensive play-by-play since retiring in 2002.

Just like that, Harwell, 88, returned to the role that made him a legend in Detroit, the gentleman broadcaster who made the Hall of Fame in Cooperstown, N.Y.

After the second inning with the Tigers' radio network, Harwell spent the third and fourth with ESPN's Jon Miller and Joe Morgan and the fifth with ESPN Radio.

When Harwell spent his stanza in his old booth,

KATHY KIELISZEWSKI

Ernie Harwell got mike time before and during Game 3 of the 2006 ALDS vs. the Yankees. Harwell worked two innings for ESPN.

seated between Dan Dickerson and Jim Price, the Tigers surged to a 3-0 lead.

"It was fun," Harwell said as he walked from WXYT-AM's booth to ESPN's TV booth.

He wore a tie and his trademark hat. His preparation was the same, making notes on his scorecard.

And one night seemed like plenty.

"That's my kind of job," he said. "I never wanted to be overworked.

"When I was working, I did every game — I missed only two in 55 years. ... I was a little reluctant to do this. But everybody says, 'You're not making a comeback. You're going to do a couple innings.' "

On ESPN, Harwell told stories, mentioned a slew of old-timers — from umpire Bill Klem to Tiger Harry Heilmann — and punched out two more hitters on called third strikes — once with the house-by-the-side-of-the-road line and once for "excessive window shopping."

"He's an icon here in Detroit, what he stands for and who he is as a man," said Tigers right-hander Jason Grilli, whose father, Steve, pitched for Detroit during the mid-1970s. "It's nice to have all the good karma going our way. I wish I could actually listen to him, too."

ORIGINALLY PRINTED OCT. 7, 2006.

A thrilling seat for the Series

BY JO-ANN BARNAS

The first inning was over, and now it was Ernie Harwell's turn to get into position. He placed his pens — one black, one blue — next to a scorecard that bore a crease down the middle. He was seated between Tigers radio play-by-play announcer Dan Dickerson and analyst Jim Price, and just after he adjusted his headset one last time, Harwell accepted a gracious introduction by Dickerson for a grateful radio audience with the words:

"Wow! What a thrill to be with you guys, and what a thrill to see World Series time again here in Michigan. It is wonderful — Mr. Verlander ready to go to work now. Jim Edmonds will be the batter. The Tigers got a run in the opening inning. They lead it 1-0 as we begin inning number two, game number one, of the 2006 World Series."

The Tigers' lead was brief; the St. Louis Cardinals came back and won. Harwell's return to the booth was brief as well; he had accepted an invitation to call one inning, the second.

But for anyone who was listening, the Hall of Fame announcer made it count.

He even had the chance to revive a trademark call — "Might be, and it is, long gone!" to describe Cardinals third baseman Scott Rolen's home run in the top of the inning.

Back on the air after a commercial break, Harwell displayed his humble sense of humor: "Last half of the second inning, the boy-announcer-now-retired Ernie Harwell, along with Dan Dickerson and Jim Price. This is exposure, it may be indecent exposure, but I'm going to keep trying no matter what they say."

After three straight outs by the Tigers, Harwell bid Dickerson, Price and his radio audience farewell.

Outside the door to the booth, Harwell said: "This is a poignant moment for me, to have a World Series back here and see the enthusiasm and baseball fever returning. I think everybody knew it would some day, but we didn't know when. It's been a long wait."

In his hand was a scorecard.

"Just a lineup," he said. "I don't deal with lots of stats and stuff."

ORIGINALLY PRINTED OCT. 22, 2006.

'07 encore results in easy Tigers' romp

BY JOHN LOWE

In Ernie Harwell's last several years as a Tigers announcer, the club finished with a losing record. On May 24, 2007, Harwell returned to broadcasting for a game in which the first-place Tigers added to their American League lead in runs in a 12-0 romp over the Los Angeles Angels.

"I think their lineup is fantastic," Harwell said after serving the first of a two-day substitution for Rod Allen as the analyst on FSN Detroit. "They've got so many guys who can break out. If one isn't hitting, two others are. They all hit home runs, from the leadoff man down to the No. 9 hitter. They're going to be hard to contain, I think.

"The nice thing is they get a lot of two-strike hits and two-out hits, and they're a lot more patient than they've been in the last couple of years."

Added Harwell: "It's a great thrill for me to see the spirit that has returned to Michigan that the Tigers have engendered. Jim Leyland deserves a lot of credit for it. I think everybody in the state loves the Tigers, and they're back to show everybody that baseball is a great game."

So great that a blowout like the one against the

Angels still can have a turning point.

"When (Jeremy) Bonderman got out of the first inning (bases loaded, none out), that was a crucial part of the game," Harwell said. "If he walks another guy or gives up a two-base hit, the whole game changes."

Harwell also subbed for Allen four years ago, in the first year of his retirement. He was asked how this assignment reminds him of what he likes most about broadcasting.

"It reminds me that it's a real challenge to do a decent broadcast," Harwell said. "I just admired the way that Mario (Impemba) did the play-by-play. He's such a great professional. It was wonderful to work with him and let him do the heavy lifting."

If you need a guest, why not get the best?

ORIGINALLY PRINTED MAY 25, 2007.

BREAKING 90

INDEX

I N D E X

INDEX

INDEX

INDEX

W

Z

Y

About the author

Ernie Harwell was born in Washington, Ga., on Jan 25, 1918. He began his career in radio and television in 1940 and has been broadcasting major league baseball since 1948. He retired after the 2002 Tigers season. He has written five other books — "Stories From My Life in Baseball," "Tuned to Baseball," Diamond Gems," "The Babe Signed My Shoe" and "Life After Baseball." He lives in Novi, Mich., with his wife, Lulu.